REDEEMING
T**HE**ME

THE CHRISTIAN WALK
IN A HURRIED WORLD

REDEEMING THE TIME

THE CHRISTIAN WALK
IN A HURRIED WORLD

PHILIP D. PATTERSON, PH.D.

COLLEGE PRESS
PUBLISHING COMPANY
Joplin, Missouri

Library of Congress Cataloging-in-Publication Data

Patterson, Philip.
   Redeeming the time: the Christian walk in a hurried world /
Philip D. Patterson.
      p.   cm.
   Includes bibliographical references.
   ISBN 0-89900-726-0
   1. Time management—Religious aspects—Christianity. I. Title.
BV4598.5.P38   1995
248.4—dc20   94-44044
                                                CIP

See then that ye walk circumspectly,
not as fools but as wise,
Redeeming the time,
because the days are evil.

Eph. 5:15-16 (KJV)

For
BAILEY B. MCBRIDE

While others have concentrated on *time spending* or *time stretching*, you have chosen to excel in *time sharing*, and because of that, you have made a world of difference.

TABLE OF CONTENTS

INTRODUCTION

ARE YOU "TIME CRUNCHED?"

I saw the question above in a magazine, and couldn't resist taking the quiz. According to the editors of *American Demographics* magazine, if you agree with more than three statements on the list below, consider yourself "time crunched." The statements are followed by a percentage of respondents who agreed with each one in a survey of 1010 U.S. adults sponsored by Hilton Hotels in January of 1991. See how many of the statements below describe your life. Compute your score. If you're under three, give this book to someone who needs it. If you're three or over then read on.

Statement (% of Americans who agree)

1. I often feel under stress when I don't have enough time (43%).
2. When I need more time, I tend to cut back on my sleep (40%).
3. At the end of the day, I often feel that I haven't accomplished what I set out to do (33%).
4. I worry that I don't spend enough time with my family

or friends (33%).
5. I feel that I'm constantly under stress — trying to accomplish more than I can handle (31%).
6. I feel trapped in a daily routine (28%).
7. When I'm working long hours, I often feel guilty that I'm not at home (27%).
8. I consider myself a workaholic (26%).
9. I just don't have time for fun anymore (22%).
10. Sometimes I feel that my spouse doesn't know who I am anymore (21%).

Your score: _____

So you'll know something about me, my score on the survey is about six and a half. I completely agree with at least five of the statements and another three are probably partially true. My wife might put the total even a little higher. But lest you think I'm not the one to write this book, consider the example of Paul. When he wrote to the Philippians about wanting to know Christ and to share in His sufferings, death and resurrection, he adds in the next verse:

> *Not that I have already obtained all this, or have already been made perfect,* but I press on to take hold of that for which Christ Jesus took hold of me (Phil. 3:12).

From the psalmist David to the apostle Paul, God has used "imperfect" messengers because they're what He has available. And though I'm not in a league with those writers, I've run through enough airports and worked through enough nights to be qualified as a messenger about walking the Christian walk in a world now running at breakneck speed.

I discovered several things in writing this manuscript and I'll reveal several of them as you read through the chapters. But the thing that surprised me the most was discovering that I really didn't know God. I knew *of* God, but I didn't *know* God. And the reason why I didn't know Him is found in David's statement: "Be still and know that I am God" (Psalm 46:10). I simply hadn't been still long enough lately. Consequently, the God I once knew well had become more of a stranger to me. One of my goals for the next year is to fix this problem with a steady diet of prayer and quiet time.

I also discovered I had some good time habits and some poor ones. While I was good at *redeeming* the time (Eph. 5:15 KJV), I was not all that great at choosing "what is better" (Luke 10:42). I was always busy, yet I left some areas of my responsibilities undone or poorly done. In talking to other Christians, I found that problem was hardly unique to me. In fact, since Christians have all the normal time pressures of society *and* a commitment to Christian service, it is almost *inevitable* that the Christian life will be a full and even busy one.

We aren't the first generation to think we live in a hurried world. More than 150 years ago, Alexander Campbell wrote that "This present age is not an age given to devotion. Men have not the time to meditate, to pray, to examine themselves. They have too many newspapers to read, too many political questions to discuss, too much business to transact." We didn't invent the hurried-up life, we just seem to have perfected it.

Historian Will Durant once observed that "no man who is in a hurry is quite civilized." You need only to observe human behavior on a crowded freeway or a rush hour subway station to agree to that. But I'm more concerned with the possibility that no one who is constantly in a hurry can be fully Christian, either. How do I balance the demands of a Christian life with the command to "Be still?"

This book is written from the perspective of one who doesn't have that delicate balance worked out yet, but one who is trying. In this book you'll find some of the best literature on time management put into the light of the scriptures. To help me make the best use of my time, several people have helped along the way: my wife, Linda, my secretary, Susie Rodman, my research librarian, Tamie Willis, and my editor, John Hunter. Thank you all.

In the end, I hope something in this book will help you answer the important question asked by Peter: "What kind of people ought you to be?" (2 Peter 3:11). In its context, it's a question he poses right after reminding his readers of the certainty of the judgment to come. If we believe in a *judgment* day, Peter says, it should affect how we live *every* day. What kind of people ought we to be? We ought to be a people who know how to properly use, appreciate and enjoy one of God's most precious gifts: time.

*"An inch of time cannot be bought
by an inch of gold."*
Chinese proverb

CHAPTER ONE

INVESTING YOUR "TALENT" OF TIME

"Time is money." It's one of our most enduring clichés. Yet, unlike many cultural "truisms," this one happens to be true. Time is valuable today for the same reason that gold, salt, jewels and other commodities have been valuable over the centuries — its scarcity.

At the time of Jesus' ministry, gold was more precious than any other commodity. That's why so many of his teachings centered on material wealth and how to deal with it. He looked into the hearts of men and saw what was most precious and demanded some or even all of it (Matt. 19:21). Jesus taught in a culture that knew little of time scarcity. They lived their lives governed by the seasons and the religious festivals. Yet given the value of time today, I am convinced that Jesus' teachings on money are equally applicable to time. And if He were here today, He would be teaching about both.

Go through the teachings of Jesus on money and substitute the principal of time. See how many of them still apply. Try this one from the Sermon on the Mount, "For where your treasure is, there will your heart be also" (Matt. 5:21). Now substitute the notion of time into the passage:

"For where your time is spent, there will your heart be also." Works, doesn't it? If I live to work, my heart is there. If I live to fish, my heart is there also, even when my body is somewhere else.

Consider the parable of the talents in Matthew 25. What if that commodity which Jesus gave each of the three men was simply a unit of time to do with as he pleased? Suppose the unit of time was a lunar month. Suppose to one He gave five months, to one three months, to one a single month off from their regular lives (like an ancient sabbatical) to invest in any way they saw fit. And at the end of that time, He wanted to see a return on that time.

When Jesus returns as the Master returned in the parable, if time is the "talent" that he has endowed each with, what will your return be? It's a logical question. Time as a "talent" matches all the criteria of the parable: everyone has some of it (24 hours in a day) though some ultimately have more (long lives versus short lives). Hardly any other commodity fits the parable as well. We're not all equally endowed with intelligence, opportunity, health, money, etc. But *for today*, we are all equally endowed with the "talent of time." And in the end, *how* we use what we are given, not *how much* we were given, will be the a key determiner in whether we hear the words "Well done, good and faithful servant!" or those awful words, "You wicked lazy servant!" As the ancient saying goes, to live well is better than to live long.

Jesus knew that not all uses of time were equal in their value. As He sat in the house of Mary and Martha, He talked with Mary as Martha hurried about the house to prepare a proper meal for the Master. Imagine the scene. Jesus is in your house. Would you drop everything and listen to His teachings, or would you try to get the cobwebs out of the corners before He happens to see them? Mary chose the former, Martha chose some version of the latter. Martha complained to Jesus that Mary wasn't helping. But Jesus knew His time was short and that Mary had chosen well.

Centuries later, time spent with Jesus is still in short supply. We will spend a third of our lives at work or school, another third resting from our labor. What is left is often squandered. The average American will spend *nine and a half years* watching television over a lifetime. Yet if you attend worship *every Sunday* until the age of sixty-five you will spend only *four and a half months* in worship. Is it any wonder that Jesus told Martha that Mary had chosen "the better part" when she chose to sit at His feet?

Take a look at the two groups in the parable of the sheep and the goats also found in Matthew 25. The difference in the groups was not a matter of opportunity. Both groups had equal opportunities to feed the hungry, clothe the naked or visit the imprisoned. Yet one group seized the opportunities while the other group did not. And the most interesting thing about the parable is that the individuals who were on the right hand *couldn't even remember the acts of kindness for which they were being rewarded.* To them, the acts were so natural that they scarcely noticed that they were doing the Master's work.

To me, that says more about their lifestyle than the fact that they performed the good works. They not only did them as a natural part of their days, they proceeded to forget them and go on to other things. Their time was not their own — it was consumed in helping others.

It is no coincidence that in the parable of the Good Samaritan found in Luke 10, the two men who passed by the wounded man were probably both on their way to do good works. But the priest and the Levite in the parable made an error that many of us make each day: they confused their busyness and their business. The priest and the Levite should have been about the business of doing good. But the busyness of the day got in the way of the business they were called out by God to do. As a Christian, I am in the business of conducting my life in a manner "worthy of the gospel of Christ" (Phil. 1:27). My challenge is to not let my busyness get in the way. The use of the word "conduct" is interesting here. Have you ever watched an orchestra conductor? He's the one in control. He emphasizes the parts that he wishes to emphasize and relegates to the background the parts that he considers less important.

When is the last time you felt like a conductor when it comes to your daily schedule? Are you in control? Can you pull out the important parts at will and sublimate all the "counter-melodies" to their proper role? Notice the order of Philippians 1:27. Until you can become a conductor of your own life, you can't advance to the rest of the command in that passage — standing firm and contending for the faith. Until we can get a handle on the *quantities* of our worldly obligations, we cannot hope to live the *quality* of spiritual life suggested by Paul. And the first step is to recognize the difference between our busyness and our business.

For an example we need only to look at the life of Jesus in the first few chapters of the gospel of John. Several things are striking in these chapters. First, the repeated use of the phrase "the next day" (1:29; 1:35; 1:43) or "the third day" (2:1) makes me realize how little is recorded by John in light of our Twentieth Century standards of cramming something into every minute. The point is not that Jesus *wasted* time, but that He *spent* time, and lots of it, on each individual.

Second, you can see a lot of spontaneity in these chapters, a willingness to get off the schedule if the needs dictated. The time that Jesus spent in the town of the Samaritan woman (4:43) is an excellent example of this flexibility. Jesus and His apostles were quite likely traveling on the west side of the Jordan to avoid the crowds. Yet, seeing the responsive crowds, a stop for water and provisions became a two-day stay.

Third, you see what is, I think, a purposeful imprecision in timekeeping. Compared to the book of Acts, where we know the hour of the sermon on Pentecost or the hour of Cornelius's vision, John's account has a charming lack of precision in its timekeeping. We see phrases like "after this

. . . they stayed for a few days" (2:12) and "when it was almost time" (2:13). We read that Jesus and the disciples retreated into the Judean countryside where they spent "some time" (3:22). Both chapters five ("Some time later") and six ("Some time after this") begin with this laissez-faire attitude towards time.

But lest you think that Jesus did not maximize His time, consider this: in three years, He equipped tax collectors, fishermen and the like to carry on his mission after His ascension. That was His business, and He didn't let busyness get in the way, even if it meant missing an opportunity to reach Lazarus before he died. Read the gospels carefully and you will see that they are filled with examples of Jesus going against traditions of time well-spent. He healed on the Sabbath. He took time out of his interaction with the crowds to pay attention to the children. He gave private audiences to sinners.

In times of war, Army hospitals close to the front lines are forced to perform triage on the masses of wounded that come in all at once. The term triage, well known to viewers of the popular television series M*A*S*H, is French for "prioritizing" or more literally, "picking out." In the battlefield application, those performing the triage separate the wounded into three groups: those who will die even with medical attention, those who can be saved with immediate medical care, and those will survive even without immediate attention. It is to the middle group that the surgeons turn their initial efforts.

Once we determine what business we are in as children of God, we can perform similar triage on our schedules. On one level are the things we can't change no matter how much effort we put into them. On another level are things that we can change if we try. On the third level are the trivial things that don't matter much one way or another.

It is my contention that worries about health fall into this first category of triage — we can't do much about it and worry won't help. On the other hand, much of our parenting, evangelism and other responsibilities fall into that crucial second category — we can have a real impact if we are there and ready at the right time. It is the third category — the trivial — that has us held captive when many of the opportunities to do good arrive. And what I include in that third category might be controversial. In my opinion, in that trivial group of time-consuming activities is our earning a living. Look at the words of Jesus in Matthew 7 when He reminds us that the same God who clothes the grass of the field and feeds the birds of the air will do the same for us. Whether or not I am rich seems to be irrelevant to God, and some teachings of scripture seem to indicate that wealth could even be a hindrance to my salvation.

Our secular culture has pushed how we make a living and how well we live into the critical category, and extracted huge sums of time in the process. Even many of our churches have blurred the lines between a successful Christian walk and a financially successful life in the messages from their pulpits. And we as Christians have never run counter-cultural and said "No!"

The problem is our total unwillingness to settle for less. Nowhere in the American culture is the concept of cutting back revered and held up as a model. Instead, because we want the best for our families we are forced to join a race like rats on a treadmill in order to just stay up. Recently, Priority Management of Seattle has found that more than half of all workers routinely exceed the forty hour work week by ten hours or more. Ironically, while most were working these longer hours for the good of their family, eighty-five percent of them worried about leading a more balanced life with time for family, hobbies and volunteer work. Only two percent thought they were juggling their lives successfully.[1]

Our time is our most precious commodity that we have to invest. Peter puts this in perspective when he reminds us that "Since everything will be destroyed in this way, what kind of people ought you to be?" He then answers his own question: "You ought to live holy and godly lives" (2 Peter 3:11).

God gave me something valuable when he gave me today. Tomorrow he may come and ask to see the return on today and all the yesterdays he has given as well. And the return he will look for is not in the perishable things that will be destroyed by his return, but in the imperishable treasures stored up where moths cannot corrupt and thieves cannot steal. Remember, where my time is, my heart will be also.

A final illustration comes from the burgeoning popularity of cram courses for bar exams and those exams that get students into competitive graduate school. They amaze me. How can one go to law school for four years or college for four years and need those cram courses to do well? The answer is simple: the instructors know the form the test will take, and they teach to the probabilities of the test. The result is a quick course that majors in what is likely to count and counts all else as trivial — a form of triage.

As Christians, we know precisely what form the "final" with God will take. The parable of the sheep and goats in Matthew 25 gives us a glimpse of the test, and success is nowhere to be found in the criteria. How much of our time are we using to prepare ourselves and our children for the only test that will ever count? It will be pass/fail. We will either hear "Well done good and faithful servant" or "You wicked, lazy servant," depending in great part how we have invested God's gift of time.

Endnote

1. Anne B. Fisher, "Welcome to the Age of Overwork." *Fortune*, November 30, 1992, pp. 64-71.

"My days are swifter
than the weaver's shuttle"
Job 7:6

CHAPTER TWO
_____

HAVE YOU GOT THE TIME?

In suburban Chicago, children who want to sit on Santa's lap at one suburban mall can book a five minute slot with Kris Kringle to avoid standing in line. In Scottsdale, Arizona, a golf course takes steps to assure that everyone playing finishes in four hours — about two hours faster than the pace of many golf courses. In San Francisco, a restaurant offers computers with Internet at the tables so diners can check their E-mail over lunch.

Forget work for a moment. It seems that even our breaks are becoming subject to "timelock,"[1] where demands on time become so overwhelming that it becomes impossible to wring time out of the day for everything. Like gridlock on a crowded freeway that traps us in our cars, timelock ends up trapping us in a crowded schedule. Other new words and phrases such as "hypertime," "time deepening" and "time stuffing" are popping up to describe how we can wring more activities out of our 24-hour day. In an era where computers are programmed to ensure they will work on a second task during any micro-seconds left unused by the first task, it often seems that humans are running under the same set of instructions.

Pollsters tell us: "Time may become "the most precious commodity in the land." Researchers claim: "Time could end up being to the 1990s what money was to the 1980s."[2] Authors remind us with titles such as *Time Dollars: A Currency for the 90s* what we already knew: time is not only money, but today the two are almost indistinguishable.[3]

The evidence can be seen in our spending patterns. People who have an ample supply of our society's second most valuable commodity — money — spend a lot of it in pursuit of more time. Fewer than a quarter of all families now match the "Ozzie and Harriet" model of a nuclear family with a full-time homemaker and wage-earning father — down 50 percent in a decade. Subsequently more families and their children are having to cope with changing roles and less time.

Those coping mechanisms include paying to do things we once did ourselves. More than half of all meals are now purchased outside the home. *American Demographics* has called the take-out restaurant the "ultimate cooking appliance" of the 1990s.[4] Fast foods, meals ready to heat and serve, microwave ovens, lawn care services, and weekly maid service are but a few of the ways that money can be spent to gain valuable time. And day after day we gladly make the transaction: "You cook my dinner (clean my pool, change my sheets, etc.) and give me back my time to enjoy it, and I'll reward you with money."

However, this trend has a down side. These chores that are being contracted out have traditionally had a "binding" function in the family as well. Demographer Peter Morrison warns that families that contract out everything soon resemble an "enterprise" more than a family. The activities like yard work or dishwashing that once brought a family together or served as the basis for earning allowances are now either automated or contracted out.

Often the ways in which we buy time are so subtle as to go unnoticed. As a child, I remember watching my mother cut up chicken to fry for dinner. On those rare occasions today which my family cooks our own chicken we buy it already cut into pieces. It occurs to me that my children have never seen *anyone* cut up a chicken. They probably think it falls into eight pieces when the feathers are plucked. And cut-up (skinned and boned) chicken is just the tip of the iceberg of what merchants offer time-starved Americans. Look in your pantry. If you are typical, half of the items there — both food and appliances — did not exist even two decades ago. And the reason for most of these new items has little to do with nutrition. Most were developed for their convenience.

However, a funny thing happened in our race to acquire more time-saving devices: we ran out of time to use them all. Americans today own and consume roughly twice what they did in 1958, yet they report less free time and less satisfaction. Forty years ago, fewer than five percent of all homes had dishwashers and clothes dryers. None had microwaves. Now that we have acquired all of these things and more, something has filled the time that they freed up. And that something is longer work hours to pay for our affluence.

After succeeding in the late 1930s to achieve a national standard of the 40-hour, five-day work week, American workers four decades later gave back that hard-earned concession willingly to pay for the "good life" that long-hour jobs allowed. According to one poll, the *average* American work week jumped from under 41 hours to almost 47 hours in the past two decades. For professionals it climbed to *52 hours*. Leisure time during that same period took a beating, shrinking by 37%.

Meanwhile, advertisers sold a media image of "the good life" since they had much to gain by the higher incomes that long hour jobs brought. If Americans started working shorter hours and had less discretionary income, the result could be disastrous for most advertisers. So, industry spends $50 billion per year in the media to preach the gospel of conspicuous consumption, encouraging Americans to consume more goods and services.

As the amount of work we did increased, its role in our lives changed. Repeatedly, television shows ranging from "Murphy Brown" to "L.A. Law" showed workplaces functioning as substitutes for home and workers substituting as surrogate family. For many, work has taken on the traditional functions of religion by providing an answer to such basic questions as "Who am I?" and "Where am I going?" These questions that were historically answered at worship are now answered at work.

The shift towards longer hours has not only changed the way we work, but the way we play. With exhausting careers to contend with, the last thing we want is to be intellectually or creatively challenged during our leisure time. In 1938, during the height of the 40-hour work week, the most popular ways to spend an evening were reading, watching movies and dancing. In 1986, the highest honors went to television, followed by resting, relaxing and reading. No one even mentioned resting or relaxing as a favorite leisure-time activity in the 1938 survey. As work became more challenging, our play became more passive. Consequently, by the mid-1990s, research from the Academy of Leisure Sciences indicated that Americans were losing the skills necessary to get the most benefit from their free time, opting instead for the immediate gratification of television.[5]

As a result of our exhausting days combined with our tendency to relax in front of the television, we are, as a nation, losing an entire set of skills that once was the product of "down time." Such things as handwritten letters, cross-stitched family trees, embroidered quilts and hand-carved furniture were once prized for generations. Now these time-consuming skills are almost lost to the rapid pace of modern life.

The following illustration drives home the problem. Early in his brief run as host of a late night talk show,

Dennis Miller told an interviewer that he had asked his friend Johnny Carson "when do the weekends get long enough to recover from the week?" One doesn't have to have a high profile television job to identify with the statement. As we approach our weekends increasingly exhausted, hobbies and family activities get postponed or forgotten in exchange for rest from our exhaustion.

It didn't have to be that way. Progress could have brought with it more leisure, and indeed many articles in the 1950s predicted a more leisurely lifestyle. But as a nation, America has opted to take every "productivity dividend" since the end of World War II as a raise in pay rather than a reduction in work time. The productivity dividend is what is left over when you can perform the same amount of work in Year B as you did in Year A in less time. You can either keep working, making more products and more money for your employer (who will pass it on to you) or you could go home early, your work done.

As a nation, we have chosen the route of more money and less time off. No one took a vote. Workers simply looked at the things that a raise could buy and gladly turned every productivity dividend into a raise for four decades. Juliet Schor in *The Overworked American* says that if those same dividends had been applied to time off every year since the end of World War II, America would now enjoy a four-hour work day or a six-month work year *with full pay*.[6]

Having chosen the route of riches, workers turned their yearly raises into more purchasing, much of it on credit. Then in a perverse twist, productivity flattened and the dividends went away. Companies cut back and many Americans had to take a pay cut just to ensure job security. Others saw their work loads increase dramatically when they were fortunate enough to survive a corporate cutback. And the things purchased on credit? Money was still owed on them with less time left to enjoy them. Second jobs became the norm to support lifestyles bloated beyond the capacity of a single paycheck.

Eventually, the "good life" came to a screeching halt for many with the corporate cutbacks of the 1980s and 1990s. According to a recent American Management Association report, 39 percent of 1,084 organizations surveyed cut their work forces in the previous twelve months. Thirty-five percent did so during the same period the year before. Those remaining are expected to pick up the slack, taking on more responsibility and putting in longer hours.[7]

Subsequently the bulk of us found work in one of two types of jobs, according to Schor. The "fortunate" who kept their positions were left with long hour, well-paying, high-stress jobs. The ones who were cut usually found low paying service sector jobs, where they quickly found that one well-paying (and now lost) smokestack job paid better than two marginal service jobs. As Sylvia Hewlett comments in *When the Bough Breaks,* "Burger King simply does not pay as well as Bethlehem Steel."[8] Michael Moore's poignant and highly-acclaimed documentary film "Roger and Me" chronicled the plight of Flint, Michigan when General Motors cut back and families with once comfortable existences had to scramble harder to make far less money.

With that historical perspective, let's turn to the scriptures. Perhaps the most unusual fact about this valuable commodity known as time is that it is spread absolutely equal throughout society. The millionaire and the homeless both have 24 hours in a day, with the total of their days numbered by God. Nothing can change that. Jesus assured us of that in Matthew 6:27 when He asked, "Who of you by worrying can add a single hour to his life?"

The answer to Christ's rhetorical question is "no one." We all know someone that is taking hours (or more likely, years) from his life by worry and stress. But none of us can point to a single individual that worried her way into an extra hour of life. Even the miracles of modern medicine have done little to extend the average life expectancy beyond the Biblical "threescore and ten" (Psalm 90:10).

So what is left are those who use their allotted time well and those who squander it. Like any investment, time can be invested and return dividends and wasted to return nothing. Time is akin to the bread "cast upon the waters" in Ecclesiastes 11:1. Invested, it comes back again and again. Time spent in a flower garden should come back annually in beautiful flowers. Time spent in parenting should return in children who remain in the Lord (Prov. 22:6). Time spent in fellowship with friends should come back in memories. Time spent in exercise should result in better health.

Time is indeed the most valuable commodity of our day and God wants and deserves only the best. Since the days of Cain and Abel, God has wanted only the best gift. That's why Jesus commended the two coins from the widow (Mark 12:43), probably to the astonishment of his apostles, while He made no comment about the many who had given from their wealth.

We're living in an era in which it is easier (not *easy*, but *easier*) to tithe from our incomes than it is to tithe from our time. But when we give from our fiscal abundance, we stand in danger of making the mistake of Cain — offering God what is second best. The next time you reach into your pocket to give something of value to your church, try this. Pass over the pocket with the wallet, skip the pocket with the checkbook and reach for the pocket with the day planner. Find some time to give and give it liberally. Then you will begin to appreciate the magnitude of the gift that the widow gave.

God's people are called to be holy. The word for holy, *hagios*, did not mean to the New Testament reader "pious" or "righteous" as it does today. It meant "separate," as in separated out from sin. And when we are called to be holy (Rom. 12:1; Col. 1:22 and 1 Pet. 2:5) that means we are called to be separate from the ways of the world. And a part of that separation must be reflected in how we spend our most valuable commodity — our time.

The good news is that we are not called to a monastic life of denial to satisfy God. The secret is to align our life with Him, and the days and hours fall into place. In Ecclesiastes, Solomon speaks of two lifestyles: life "under the sun" and life "under heaven." As Christians, we're not living a "meaningless" life "under the sun" (Eccl. 2:14). We're living a life "under heaven" (Eccl. 3:1) where *there is a time and a season for everything*. The message of Ecclesiastes is that if our desire is to live for eternity, then our expenditure of time will align itself into the will of God, *even when much of it consists of routine, everyday activities*. Read the list in Ecclesiastes chapter three for proof. Conversely, if our desire is to live only for the here and now — we will be forever "chasing after the wind" (Eccl. 2:14) *even when engaging in many of the same activities*.

The ability of God to consecrate even our everyday activities is seen in a quote by songwriter Frances R. Havergal who once wrote in her dairy: "Writing is praying with me." As a writer, I like that quote. However, if your life is fully consecrated to God, you could substitute a variety of words there. That attitude is reflected in Havergal's most famous consecration hymn written more than a century ago:

> "Take my life and let it be,
> Consecrated, Lord to Thee.
> Take my moments and my days,
> Let them flow in ceaseless praise."

The challenge is one of lifestyle, not clock hours. I'm comforted by the thought that just like the little boy's loaves and fishes, there's no gift of time too small to offer Jesus. He wants even the moments. But I'm perplexed by the thought that the same Lord told one young man to leave his unburied father to follow Him and told another to sell everything he had and follow Him. He wants the days as well. Our challenge is to be equally ready to offer both to Him.

Endnotes

1. Ralph Keyes, *Timelock* (New York: HarperCollins, 1991).

2. Nancy Gibbs, "How America has run out of time." *Time*, April 24, 1989, pp. 57-61, 66-67.

3. Edgar Cahn and Jonathan Rowe, *Time Dollars* (Emmaus, PA: Rodale Press, 1991).

4. Harry Balzer, "The Ultimate Cooking Appliance." *American Demographics,* July, 1993, pp. 40-44.

5. "We Get Little Satisfaction from Being Sofa Spuds." *Atlanta Constitution*, April 5, 1993, Sec. E, p. 1.

6. Juliet P. Schor, *The Overworked American* (New York: Basic Books, 1991).

7. Amy Saltzman, *Downshifting* (New York: HarperCollins, 1991) p. 40.

8. Sylvia Hewlett, *When the Bough Breaks* (New York: Basic Books, 1991), p. 57.

CHAPTER THREE

RUNNING ON OVERTIME: HOW WE BECAME SLAVES TO THE CLOCK

Historian Daniel J. Boorstin says that when it comes to chronicling our human accomplishments to date, we must begin by acknowledging that "the first grand discovery was time." Among God's creation, humans alone manipulate time to suit their needs. Jeremy Rifkin, author of *Time Wars,* says "Time has been our most important innovation. We have used this instrument to fashion our cultures. It is the primary socializing tool."[1]

For most of us, our adult life consists of three components — work, maintenance and leisure — each taking up roughly one third of our life. Work provides the necessities for survival. Maintenance activities — sleeping, resting, eating, grooming — restore the body to its desired state following work and get us ready to work again. The rest is leisure, the "newest" of the three components. Leisure as a concept began when workers began to work at others' bidding, literally "selling their time" to those who then sold that production for profit. When each man was no longer his own employer, it became necessary to have a system of separation between work and non-work. Leisure was born.

The ancient Greeks felt that someone with no leisure

(i.e. slaves) was not fully human. However, they had a unique definition of leisure. To the Greeks of the time of Aristotle and Plato, leisure was to the mind what rest was to the body. Indeed, our word for school is from the Greek for leisure — "schole" — since learning and leisure were synonymous to them.*

Free men have always desired leisure. Throughout antiquity and the Middle Ages the annual number of holidays (literally "holy days") was about 115.[2] Eventually that number began to fall and the possibility of exploiting workers crept in. Protection for some workers came as early as 1395 when weavers, fullers, washers, masons, carpenters and other wage earners in Paris were guaranteed by ordinance that the "working day is fixed from the hour of sunrise to the hour of sunset with meals to be taken at reasonable times." For others workers in the factories of England and the U.S. protection came much later when crusading journalists and politicians attempted to clean up the sweatshops that the industrial revolution had spawned. Early in the industrial revolution, workdays lengthened and holidays lessened. Factory and mining days were often 14 hours long and workers began to work as young as six. These uneducated and exploited workers often turned to drink as their only leisure.[3]

America was founded by a class of people who knew long work hours. The English Puritans who helped to settle early America developed what Max Weber called the "Protestant Ethic," the belief that idleness was sin and that work, pure and simple work, was virtuous for its own sake.

------

*Unfortunately, however, that time to develop the mind was made possible by abundant slave labor. In fact, both the great democracies of history — Greece and the U.S. — were built on the inexpensive labor that slavery provided. Even the writings of Paul in the New Testament acknowledge the presence of a slave class in early Christendom. The decline of slavery in the U.S. not coincidentally coincided with the decline of the time-consuming "Republic of Letters" that marked the early democracy.

The Protestant ethic made productive work the only worthwhile activity. The ethic was so widespread that King James I in 1618 had to promote from the pulpits of England his "Book of Sports" to get people interested in leisure activities on holidays.

In *Keeping Watch*, Michael O'Malley describes the underlying Biblical basis for the Protestant work ethic.[4]

> In the Judeo-Christian heritage, time has always belonged to God. According to Genesis, God began time by dividing light from dark and setting the heavens moving. And since Adam and Eve's eviction from Eden, God's ownership has demanded hard labor — time on earth must be spent working, to earn our daily bread. If you believe God intended you to work, then it follows that the harder you work, the more you please God. Time in this sense is like a loan from God: men and women have an obligation to use it wisely, to "improve the time," as the Puritans put it.

An example of this attitude is seen in a diary of Esther Burr, daughter of Puritan minister Jonathan Edwards. Though she frequently complained in her journal about the daily grind of her domestic labors, she wrote: "But I must submit, my time is not my own but God's." O'Malley claims that by acknowledging the origin and ownership of time in God, Calvinists were led to reorganize their work and life, in order to "redeem the time," thus showing their respect for God's gift of time by scrupulously saving and using it with piety and care.

Outside this curious sector of Puritans, other attitudes towards time evolved as the industrial revolution took hold. In the Nineteenth Century, time changed from a phenomenon rooted in nature and God ("apparent time") to an arbitrary, abstract quantity based in machines called clocks ("mean time"). Apparent time is the type of time that Abraham lived on. Jesus and his disciples lived on apparent time as well and to understand apparent time helps to enlighten some of the language of the gospels.

The ancient Hebrews of the Old Testament period divided the day into parts — morning, noon, and evening, but probably had no concept of hours. It is thought that while in Babylonian exile, the Jews learned the concept of hours as the twelfth part of a day. With the concept of an "hour," it was now possible to know about how long it had been since sunup or how long it would be until sundown. Apparent time was not very useful for measuring *durations* of time, such as half an hour, but was sufficient for pegging where one was in a day.

Apparent time is evident throughout the gospels and Acts. For instance, the disciples were said to have been sober on Pentecost since it was only the third hour of the day — about nine a.m. — the day having begun at six a.m. Jesus met the Samaritan woman at the well at the sixth hour. She was apparently doing her mid-day gathering of water at a spring outside the city when she met Him. Though He had plenty of time left to travel on that day, He stayed to teach the receptive Samaritans. Scripture also reveals that it was about the ninth hour, or the middle of the afternoon, when Jesus died, making the darkening of the skies an unmistakable phenomenon for anyone in Jerusalem on that day.

An important element of apparent time was how quickly one event followed another, an early attempt to establish cause and effect. For that reason, the King James Version of the Bible was filled with "straightway" passages, translated "immediately" by more modern versions. It is used to describe the healing of a leper (Mark 1:42), the restoring of sight to a blind man (Matt. 20:34) and most significantly the crowing of the cock right after Peter's third denial of Christ (Luke 22:60).

According to O'Malley, the change from apparent time to mean time, from telling approximate time by the sun to telling time with clocks, was more than just a superficial change — it was a change in ownership of the commodity of time. The original purpose of clocks seems to have been to tell time at night, or on a cloudy day when the sundial was not appropriate to the task. The first profession or calling to embrace the clock seems to have been monks who used timekeeping devices to signal the times of prayer.

However, the invention soon took on more uses and an even greater significance. Philosopher Lewis Mumford has noted that "With the invention of the clock, eternity ceased to serve as the measure and focus of human events."[5] He also notes that with their clocks, humans have progressed from being time keepers to time savers and now to time servers.

Originally, the first mechanical clocks told "mean time," an approximation of "sun time." At its extremes, mean time could be off by as many as sixteen minutes from the high noon of the sun, depending on the season. As commerce and rail travel required that each community could no longer have its own "noon," mean time needed to be standardized. Since most people were accustomed to taking their time from an instrument other than the sun, it was a short step towards standardizing time so that the instruments all read the same. This was accomplished on Sunday, November 18, 1830, the "day of two noons," orchestrated by the railroads and approved by most major cities served by them. It was the first time in history that time which originated from God was treated as a fungible commodity by humans.

Standard time amounted to a reconstruction of authority. By supplanting nature and God with clocks and watches, standard time replaced religious guidelines for dividing up the day, O'Malley claims.[6] The shift required that humans wrestle with larger issues: "Was time a natural phenomenon, rooted in religion? Was it subject to mastery by men?" How one answered these questions was greatly affected by whether one considered time something to be possessed or "redeemed." Soon, O'Malley claims, "the clock tended to become the thing it represented — clocks became not imitations or transcripts of time, but time itself."[7]

The publishing industry in America shows both our historical and contemporary fascination with time and the Puritanical imperative to save it. The second book published in America was an almanac, at Cambridge in either 1638 or 1639. The main attraction of colonial almanacs were the solar and lunar timetables. The timetables offered the precise hours and minutes of the rising of the sun and moon, high and low tides, eclipses, and the movements of the major stars. Ben Franklin's *Poor Richard's Almanac* contained several quotations about time including the famous "Time is money" axiom.

An early *McGuffey's Reader* shows the seriousness of time stewardship in the ditty "Pretty bee, will you come and play with me?" asked the Idle Boy. But the serious-minded bee replied, "No, I must not be idle, I must go and gather honey." Rebuffed, the idle boy asked a dog, a bird, and a horse in turn, but each was righteously busy. "What, is nobody idle?" the boy asked. "Then little boys must not be idle." So he "made haste, and went to school, and learned his lesson very well."[8]

With sales of more than 122 million, it is safe to say that many generations of school children read the lesson of the idle boy, a recurring theme according to O'Malley. "Nineteenth-century schoolbooks linked time to nature and farm work. But they nagged even more about the morality of working hard — the industry of the ant and the bee and the fecklessness of the grasshopper are ever present."[9] Schoolbooks ignored the lilies of the field, never known for their industry, O'Malley notes, in favor of the tireless bee or ant's example of diligence and frugal, orderly social organization.

More than a century after the *McGuffey's Reader*, our fascination with time continues. Stephen Covey's book *The 7 Habits of Highly Effective People* spent more than three years on the bestseller lists in the early 1990s. The *Minute* series (*Minute Manager, Minute Father,* etc.) was also a 1990s success, even spawning a *Minute Bible.* Scores of other books on time saving and time management hit the charts as well.

But while reams have been written about time *management*, relatively little has been written about time *valuing*. I am convinced that as soon as we learn to value our time, we will cease abusing it and learn to manage it. For some this could mean less time at work or in front of the television. For others it will mean more time spent on family matters. As Christians we must realize that time is life itself, and how we spend it is a measure of how grateful we are for God's precious gift of time, the "stuff" that life is made of, according to Ben Franklin.

One of Jesus' most poignant parables, about opportunity taken and opportunity lost, is found in Matthew 25. The five wise maidens were ready for the approach of the bridegroom because at some point in the wait they had used their time wisely to purchase more oil. The five foolish maidens were just as excited at the arrival of the bridegroom, but they had not used their time wisely during the wait.

In Isaiah, our lives are compared to one long wait — a wait for renewal. And what we do during that wait, and whether indeed we do wait faithfully, will determine our outcome. We are told that

> Even the youths shall faint and be weary,
> and young men shall utterly fall:
> *But they that wait upon the Lord*
> *shall renew their strength;*
> they shall mount up with wings as eagles;
> they shall run and not be weary;
> they shall walk and not faint.
>
> Isaiah 40:30-31 (KJV)

Time is the great equalizer. Wealth and health and opportunity may be distributed inequitably. Jesus acknowledged that the poor would always be with us. But rich or poor, healthy or weak, all of us have twenty-four hours in a day. My bank account of time is the same at the beginning of each day as everyone else's. Whether I will "redeem the time" and make it God's is the real issue.

For some, redeeming the time will mean repairing bad relationships or becoming a more active parent. For others, redeeming the time will mean getting rid of destructive work habits that are lengthening our days and shortening our lives. If the history of time tells us anything, it is that almost as soon as we discovered time we proceeded to control it, manipulate it and eventually abuse it. As Christians we must give control of it back to God. We need to take the attitude of David when he acknowledged to God "My times are in your hands" (Psalm 31:15) and dedicate the spending of it to Him.

Endnotes

1. Jeremy Rifkin, *Time Wars* (New York: Touchstone Books, 1987), p. 59.

2. Ida Craven cited in Steffan B. Linder, *The Harried Leisure Class* (New York: Columbia University Press, 1970).

3. Robert Kubey and Mihaly Csikszentmihalyi, *Television and the Quality of Life* (Hillsdale, NJ: Lawrence Erlbaum Associates, 1990).

4. Michael O'Malley, *Keeping Watch* (New York: Viking Penguin, 1990), p. viii.

5. Lewis Mumford cited in Neil Postman, *Amusing Ourselves to Death* (New York: Penguin, 1986).

6. O'Malley, *Keeping Watch*, p. ix.

7. *Ibid.*, p. 8-9.

8. *Ibid.*, p. 20.

9. *Ibid.*

CHAPTER FOUR

"LORD IF YOU HAD BEEN HERE": LIVING ON GOD'S SCHEDULE

Have you ever noticed that God's time schedule doesn't always jive with ours? For instance, while we are told in Isaiah 40:31 that "those who wait upon the Lord will renew their strength," *believing* in a God that can renew our strength is easier than *waiting* on Him to do it. Faith is not the problem, patience is. Similarly, while we are told in Romans 8:28 that "in all things God works for the good of those who love Him," we are not given the timetable for this equity to occur. And when the good that is promised doesn't occur within our timetable, we sometimes question the strength of our God rather than the depth of our faith.

The heroes of faith in Hebrews 11 had the right idea. Each performed deeds within his or her lifetime that made little sense in the short term. Take, for instance, Abraham and his willingness to pick up from his comfortable existence and move to a land with borders he couldn't even fathom. Abraham and the heroes of faith, we are told, "admitted that they were aliens and strangers in the earth" (Heb. 11:13) who were "looking for a better country — a heavenly one" (Heb. 11:16). In the short term, their actions looked odd, in the eternal perspective, their actions made

41

perfect sense. The secret is in the timetable.

And like those heroes of faith, we are also sojourners in this world. In realizing that our roots are not planted here, we are following the example of Christ. John 1:14 tells us that "The Word became flesh and made his dwelling among us." The Greek word there for dwell could be translated "pitched his tent." It denotes a temporary state of dwelling. Jesus was just "camping" here on earth.

And so too are we. If we look at things from that perspective, we too will begin to take actions that make more sense in the eternal timetable than the temporal one. And that is when we will begin walking by faith.

But it's not easy. Perhaps no Bible story best illustrates our tendency to wish God would follow our timetables than the story of Mary and Martha who called for Jesus when their brother Lazarus lay dying. But Jesus was slow in coming, waiting for nearly a week, and Lazarus died. We take up the story below as it might have occurred.

> The sisters had called for Jesus six days ago. At that time, their brother, Lazarus, was on his deathbed with a fever the doctors could not cure. Only thirty years old, Lazarus was now gone — the fever had taken him four days ago. And still, there was no sign of Jesus.
>
> Lazarus had lived with Mary and Martha, his unmarried sisters, and provided for them. In return, they kept his house, prepared his meals and made his clothing. The three had been friends of Jesus, following Him when He was in the region, and hosting Him in their home for a meal.
>
> The younger of the two, Mary, had a special relationship with the Master. On one occasion, when He had visited her home, Mary wanted only to sit at His feet and listen to his teachings, while Martha busily prepared the meal. Jesus had rescued her from criticism by telling Martha that Mary had made the right choice in listening to Him rather than being distracted by the preparations.
>
> But Mary was now confused. Nearly a week ago, she had

requested that Jesus hurry to their home in Bethany to heal Lazarus. She had seen Him perform numerous healings in the past, and she was certain that He would hurry to Lazarus's bed when he got the simple message, "Lord, the one you love is sick."

When He got the message, Jesus was not in the region of Judea. He had left Jerusalem after the Jews there had threatened to stone Him for blasphemy. As they attempted to seize Him and His apostles, He had crossed the Jordan to safety. It had been their closest brush with the anger of the Pharisees so far. Now Jesus received word from Mary's messenger that He must go back to where the Jews were attempting to kill Him. Yet He knew that His time on Earth was not yet up.

As Jesus contemplated the trip, He allowed two more days to pass. He weighed the grief that Mary and Martha must be bearing against the fear that His apostles would feel when he told them of His plans. Finally, He revealed his plan to the apostles, saying, "Our friend Lazarus has fallen asleep, but I am going to wake him up." Not understanding the message, and not wanting to go back into Judea, the apostles asked why Lazarus could not awake on his own. Jesus explained, "Lazarus is dead, and for your sake I am glad I was not there, so that you may believe. But let us go to him."

The apostles were frightened and shocked at His announcement. Hadn't they just escaped with their lives two days earlier? Many of them fully expected to never go back to Judea, and certainly not within days after they were nearly killed. As they pondered whether to go back to Bethany, Thomas voiced the sentiment on their minds, "Let us also go, that we may die with Him." So the Twelve, expecting the worst, turned towards Judea, the recent escape fresh on their minds.

Meanwhile, Mary's hope had turned to despair. The Lord had failed to come. Her brother had died and had been buried now for four days. She wept at her loss, and she wept from a sense of betrayal. Why hadn't He come?

He had healed total strangers. Why hadn't He come to heal one that He loved? Where was He now in their most desperate hour? She wanted answers to these questions, but could find none.

As they approached Bethany, the apostles began to feel a sense of relief. They had crossed the Jordan two days ago, and had not experienced any troubles yet. Although Bethany was only a short walk from the potential trouble in Jerusalem, it was also the home of some of the Lord's most fervent followers. Surely nothing would happen to them in Bethany.

The first resident who ran to greet them informed Jesus that Lazarus had been dead for four days, something the Lord had told the Twelve before they crossed the Jordan. They marveled at how He knew, though little about the Master surprised them anymore.

The crowds gathering at their house informed the sisters that Jesus would soon be inside the city. Martha prepared to go and meet him, but Mary chose to stay behind. What could she possibly say to Him? She had so much she wanted to say, yet it was not her place to criticize the Lord. Deep in her heart, she knew that He could have prevented the death if He had come. Why did He choose not to? Yet, did she dare ask Him such an impertinent question?

Martha, in her usual manner, went first and greeted the Lord before he entered the city. Her confrontation with Him was quick and direct. Jesus handled her questions with love and assurances, then asked for Mary. Martha went back to her home to get her younger sister.

When the sisters returned together, Jesus had still not entered the city. The apostles waited uneasily beside the road. They would have preferred being in the houses of Bethany to this open road less than two miles from the spot where they were nearly stoned in Jerusalem. Whatever Jesus was going to do, they wished that He would hurry up and do it, and take shelter with some of His followers in their homes. But they knew from experience that Jesus could not be rushed when He was dealing with people.

Mary had left her home hurriedly. As was the custom, the mourners followed her, thinking that she was going to the tomb. As Mary walked to where the Master waited, she rehearsed what she would say, changing the words with every attempt. What could she say? The question gnawed at her.

When she came to Jesus, she fell at His feet and wept. The only words that came out were not the ones she rehearsed. Instead, they were the ones directly from her heart, "Lord, if you had been here, my brother would not have died."

The words were the same ones Martha had said earlier. Yet when Mary blurted them out, crying at the Master's feet, they moved Jesus to tears. As He cried, the apostles huddled among themselves. They asked each other if any had ever seen an open display of emotion like this from Jesus. They had seen Him angry when He drove the vendors from the temple. And they had heard Him raise His voice to the Pharisees on more than one occasion, including the time a few days ago that had nearly got Him and all of them stoned to death. Yet this was a side of Jesus they hadn't seen.

The apostles wondered what it meant. A few secretly pondered if His ability to establish a kingdom would be hindered if He allowed his emotions to overrule His logic. They shouldn't even be out in the open right now, yet here they were, surrounded by the Jewish friends who had followed Mary, and Jesus was crying.

While the apostles conferred, Mary continued to weep at the feet of Jesus. After a while, Jesus asked to see the tomb, and was led there. When He got to the tomb, He ordered the stone to be rolled away. Thinking that Jesus wished to view the body, Martha reminded Him that he had been dead four days. She knew that the modest amount of spices and wrappings that they had been able to afford would only last a day or two at most in the heat.

Overruling her protest, Jesus again ordered the stone to be removed, looked up to heaven and prayed, and called out in a loud voice, "Lazarus, come out!" To the amazement of the crowd, Lazarus came out. Still clothed in burial linen, Lazarus blinked at the bright sunlight and tugged at the strips of cloth that dangled from his arms and feet, and dragged behind him as he walked.

The last person to look was Mary, who still had her face buried on Jesus's shoulder, leaning on him for support. She was afraid to look, yet wanted to. By the time that she looked, she got a glimpse of his back as some of the men from Bethany were leading him away to find him food and suitable clothing. She buried her face on His shoulder again as she wept in joy and relief at the sight of her brother.

The crowd followed Lazarus. Martha thanked Jesus and muttered an apology for her lack of faith, then turned in the direction of her home. Lazarus must be fed, and there would be an inevitable stream of visitors, meaning that she had many preparations to make, and she knew from experience that she couldn't count on Mary for any help.

The Twelve followed the crowd as well, preferring the safety of numbers to staying on the outskirts of town. They knew this miracle would keep them safe in Bethany for a while, since no one would risk crowd reaction by attempting to take Jesus now.

Soon Mary and Jesus were all alone. There, outside of Bethany, she poured her heart out to Him. Where had He been in the hour of her greatest need? Why did she not get her help from Him on her own schedule and not His?

He talked to her of life and death, resurrection and eternity. He told her that his miracles were not only to ease the current human condition, but also to glorify God and make others believe. The resurrection of Lazarus had all been a part of that plan, He said, in a way that simply healing him could have never accomplished. Her unanswered petition had not been a rejection; it simply had not fit into the eternal plan.

She was not the first to wonder where God was during a

time of crisis, He said, and she would not be the last. It was not wrong to ask the questions, He said. There is a difference between questioning and doubt. Mary had never doubted. She had simply questioned. However, He added, some questions would never be answered in this life. Faith, He said, was the only temporary relief for the burning questions of eternity.

With that, they stood and walked to the house where Martha was tending to Lazarus, and where the apostles were discussing how to convince the Master to leave under cover of dark. [1]

Each of us, I think, has both the faith of Abraham and the impatience of Mary built inside us. They tug at us daily. The everyday uncharted landmines that we encounter in working, parenting and living moral lives in the current age is a frontier as daunting as anything Abraham faced. Yet, by faith, we go on, as Abraham did because we seek a better place. But along the way come setbacks — a missed promotion, illness, the death of a loved one, financial reversal — and we take up the cry of Mary: "If only You had been here." At those times, if we are totally honest, we will often find that the problem is not a God that was too slow; it is a child of God who is in too big a hurry for everything to work out in this lifetime. Going back to our heroes of faith in Hebrews, the author says "All these people were still living by faith *when they died*. They did not receive the things promised; they only saw them and welcomed them from a distance" (Heb. 11:13). There is no guarantee that the promise of Romans 8:28, "in all things God works for the good of those who love him" will work out in this life, and indeed Biblical precedent suggests otherwise.

One of the many vivid images of Revelation is that of the dead saints who had been persecuted crying out from their waiting place under the altar: "How long?" (Rev. 6:9-10). How often have each of us been in the midst of some personal trial and wanted to know just exactly the same information: "How long?" The answer lies not in *how much time*, but *how one keeps time*. Earth was not the final destination for either the heroes of faith in Hebrews or the saints in Revelation. Nor is it the final destination for today's saints and heroes either. For that reason, earth is not the place where all things will work out for those who quietly make their way through an increasingly hostile world. Instead we hope for a better place to come at a pace determined and controlled by God.

Endnote

1. Philip Patterson, *Come Unto Me* (Joplin, MO: College Press Publishing, 1993), pp. 109-115.

"The bow, if never unbent,
will quickly break."
Ovid

CHAPTER FIVE

THE OVERACHIEVEMENT TRAP

Willard Tate in his film "How to Get What You Want and Want What You Get," makes the point that he plays golf as well as he wants, which sometimes surprises those who play with him. His point is not that he has arrived as a golfer, but that he has no burning desire to make the sacrifice necessary to take his golf game to the next level. "If I practiced an hour a day I would be better," Tate says, "but it's not worth the price. If I pay here I can't pay there." So, in truth, he plays golf as well as he wants.

The principle is true in all our lives. In any activity — work, hobbies, even parenting — we are seeking that "comfort zone" between the rigorous demands of perfection and the yawning gap of inadequacy. But for many whom we kindly label as "overachievers," finding that medium is a painful if not impossible process. They haven't learned the payment principle: if you pay too much now, you won't be able to pay later. These individuals want to excel in it all, be the superhuman juggler of career, family, church and community demands who exacts sighs of admiration from those around.

To a point, the overachiever is a Biblical principle. Jesus

noted the existence of five talent individuals and one talent individuals. Elsewhere, the scriptures warn that not every individual should seek out the role of teacher (James 3:1). In 1 Corinthians 12 Paul speaks of the many parts of the body, some having greater apparent honor than others. So the principle of excelling is certainly not contrary to scripture.

However, the idea that nothing can be average in one's life is dangerous at best and unbiblical at its worst. Sooner or later, each of us must face not one but dozens of areas in our life and say of them what Willard Tate says of his golf game, "I do that as well as I like." It is worth no more time and energy to excel in this activity.

Reaching that point in life is a step towards maturity. Aristotle taught that a virtuous life was one lived free of extremes — to seek in all areas of life the "Golden Mean." For instance, Aristotle said, bravery is a mean (or an average in our terminology) between two equally undesirable extremes. On the one extreme is the lack of bravery known as cowardice. At the other extreme is a false excess of bravery known as foolhardiness, the tendency to take on any fight no matter how costly or futile. Either extreme is undesirable and even deadly, and bravery sits as the "golden mean" between them.

It seems to me that earning a living, being a concerned parent, enjoying hobbies, even volunteer work are all "means." There are excesses and deficiencies on each side to be avoided. Don't earn so little that your family lacks, but don't spend so much time pursuing financial success that you have no time to enjoy it. Don't be a stifling parent, but don't be an unconcerned one either. Don't smother your mate, but don't ignore them either. Don't be stingy with your time but don't give too much of yourself away either. Don't lust after wealth, but don't neglect to provide for your family (1 Tim. 5:8). The list goes on and on with "golden means" or balances that we must work out in life.

To live the virtuous life described by Aristotle, he said

one had to first recognize the mean and then pursue it. Today we would call it setting priorities. In his best selling book *The 7 Habits of Highly Effective People*, Stephen Covey claims that all our activities fit into a two-by-two matrix shown below.

The Time Management Matrix

I **Urgent** **Important**	II **Not Urgent** **Important**
III **Urgent** **Not Important**	IV **Not Urgent** **Not Important**

In Quadrant I are the things that are both urgent and important. In Quadrant II are things that are not urgent but important. In Quadrant III are things that are urgent but unimportant and in Quadrant IV things are neither urgent nor important. Covey claims that because of poor planning, overcommitments and other factors, we live our lives dealing with crises in the first quadrant. The truly good time managers have found the ability, Covey says, to live life in Quadrant II dealing with important issues in a non-emergency setting.

But in our society, we sometimes applaud those who live life exclusively in Quadrant I — surrounding themselves with projects they think are urgent and important at the expense of everything else. When Jimmy Johnson took over as head coach of the NFL's worst team, the Dallas Cowboys, newspaper and magazine articles about him chronicled how he would often live in his office complex for days at a time in his quest to turn the Cowboys into a winner. Five years later, Johnson stood atop the sports world. Back to back Super Bowl trophies attested to his success. But by that time he was divorced from his wife and estranged from his grown children. Months later, he was without a job as well. He walked away from his dream job, flaming out after half a decade of pursuing winning at all costs.

Similarly, a *Newsweek* article on actor Jim Carey in the summer of 1994 chronicled how the star of two of that year's biggest films had reached the top. In it, author Kendall Hamilton stated that "He's filed for divorce from the mother of his 6-year-old girl and blames the breakup on his feverish quest for success." Carey commented on his obsession with work: "It's like a disease, it really is."[1]

The overachiever has been too long lionized by our society. While greatness deserves its due, all too often success in one area comes at the expense of another area. Some overachievers have never achieved the emotional maturity necessary to say "I am as good at golf as I want to be." They want to be better — if not better than everyone else, at least better than they are right now. And not just in one hobby like golf, but in every aspect of life.

I struggle with this aspect of Christian time management constantly — deciding what areas of life I am simply going to go for the "mean" and in what area I am going to excel. I tell myself I play basketball each day at noon to stay in shape, but those who play with me or against me will tell you that I play to win. And as I write this chapter I have staples in my right knee following my second surgery in five years. When I heal will I find the mean of bodily exercise that doesn't cross the line into bodily damage? I hope so.

I know that I'm not alone in my tendency to do everything too hard. Perhaps you can identify with this story. One physician, an award-winning runner, told me that when he had to go to the weight room to rehabilitate a running injury, he injured himself on the weight machines, competing with only himself. His orthopedic doctor, while examining the new injury asked "Just how competitive are you?" I laughed when he told me the story, but it was a knowing laugh, because at the time I was hearing the story, I was in his office to have a shoulder examined that I had injured while rehabilitating a broken ankle. We had both done the same thing: transferred our competitive natures from the roadrace or basketball court to the weight room. It's all too easy for overachievers to turn *everything* into a competition — bonuses, purchases, perfect children going to private schools — you name it, life is a competition.

Humorist Garrison Keillor writes of his desire early in his career "to write brilliant killer stuff — to write *so* brilliantly, in fact, that nobody would ever dare write humor again." I know the feeling. When I finished the second edition of my college journalism textbook I thought it would be fun if the book were the only one on the market supported by an instructor's videotape. I will admit being motivated more by competitive than pedagogical urges when I began to explore the possibility.

After securing the funding quite easily from a foundation, I started out on a six-city, cross-country semester of interviewing newsmakers and reporters in their home settings for the videotape. About halfway into the project, I could tell that the support videotape was actually going to take more of my time than the revision of the text. Six months and hundreds of hours later, I had the only textbook on the market supported by an instructor's videotape, but because I had "paid" so much for that tape, I was out of emotional "funds" to do much else for half a year. The tape will be out of date in three to four years, and I will never get back those missed opportunities to be a parent, a spouse, a Bible class teacher and everything else I put on hold for half a year. Aristotle would rightly say that I lost balance.

Overachievers have problems with the two "P's:" pride and priorities. First, they are often too proud to admit that in many areas of life good enough is sufficient. Second, they are unable to prioritize what areas of life deserve the all-out effort and what areas of life do not.

Let's return to the story of Jesus at Martha and Mary's home. While Mary sat at the feet of Jesus, Martha hurried about the kitchen to prepare a meal. Now this was no small task. Domino's Pizza delivery was out of the question. Ditto on microwaveable meals, running water, electricity or any other modern or primitive convenience. This commitment to cook a meal for Jesus was at least a couple of hours and most likely even more. Look at the cost she was willing to pay to be a good hostess. She was going to sacrifice a private audience with God incarnate for hours to prepare a single meal.

At our home we have fought the "Martha problem" over the years. I was always the one who wanted things perfect before we could invite even a few friends over for an evening of fellowship. My wife was the one who said the price was too high. And she was right. The house didn't need to be perfect to have over a few friends from church, or the youth group or a few hungry college students. To pay the price of a perfect house was to take away from something more important. It just took me a while to see it. Perhaps that's why one of the qualifications for elders is that they must be hospitable people. No one can be a hospitable person without having first wrestled with the "Martha problem" and decided that people are more important than cleaning.

As long ago as 1972 U.S. medical researchers showed that job-related stress was the surest predictor of heart disease, outdistancing smoking or diet.[2] The reason most patients don't get this information, however, is that most physicians shy away from recommending the radical life change of a job change, opting instead for the more cosmetic diet and exercise recommendations, according to internist Larry Dossey.[3]

In the U.S. we have seen the rise of such diseases as Epstein-Barr or Chronic Fatigue Syndrome affecting mostly upwardly mobile professionals with swollen glands, fever, sore joints and resulting fatigue. Though their cause isn't known, recent research indicates that addiction to work might be a factor.[4] A recent magazine article told of a people who suffer from stress-related amnesia, a rare medical condition called a "fugue state." People who push themselves beyond the limits of their ability to endure have been known to vanish unable to find their way back.[5] And from Japan is evidence of a rise in *karoshi* or "death from overwork." The victims of the disease, usually men in their forties, often have no history of health problems, yet they die suddenly from brain hemorrhages or heart attack.[6]

Others will pay an even higher price for their obsessive behavior: spiritual death. In *Working Ourselves to Death*, Diane Fassel claims that

> Spiritual bankruptcy is the final symptom of workaholism; it usually heralds a dead end. It means you have nothing left. . . I believe this aspect of workaholism is the most terrifying. It is frightening to be out of touch with a power greater than yourself. . .[7]

The problem with overachievers, perfectionists, whatever you want to call them is not the areas they excel in. The problem lies in the hidden toll that success exacts from others. Look again at another of the qualifications of elders for an example. The scripture mandates that they have believing children (Titus 1:6). In an age in which we lose nearly half of all our children by the time they reach adulthood, this requirement has fallen into disfavor as either a relic of a paternalistic era or outright legalism.

But what does this rigorous requirement really mean? I think it means that the one who would be an elder has not risen to a place of esteem through misplaced priorities. There are no hidden tolls or past due notices in the elder's life. The elder's children have not left the faith because their father was too busy leading outside the home to be a leader within. If the elder's children are faithful, the flock can be assured that those who would be its shepherds have attained a measure of balance in their lives. It tells me that at some point each one said "I play golf . . . I close deals . . . I motivate co-workers just about as well as I want." And having said that, they went home to their parenting duties. That is what I think Paul is saying in 1 Timothy 3:4 when he says that the elder must "manage his own family well."

The story is told of a conductor who was asked which was the most difficult musical instrument to play. He immediately replied, "Second fiddle. Because no one wants to do it." Part of avoiding the overachiever trap is learning the difficult craft of playing second fiddle in many of the orchestras in life so that we have the energy and resources to take center stage in the productions that matter the most.

Endnotes

1. Kendall Hamilton, "Not Another Pretty Face." *Newsweek*, July 25, 1994, pp. 50-51.

2. Anne B. Fisher, "Welcome to the Age of Overwork." *Fortune*, November 30, 1992, pp. 64-71.

3. Interviewed in Fisher, p. 71.

4. Joel F. Lehrer, and Leila M. Hover "Fatigue Syndrome." *Journal of the American Medical Association*, 259:6, (1983) pp. 842-843.

5. David Grogan, "Vanished — With a Trace." *People*, March 3, 1994, pp. 69-72.

6. Ronald Yates, "Japanese live. . .and die. . .for their work." *Chicago Tribune*, November 13, 1988, p. 1.

7. Diane Fassel, *Working Ourselves to Death* (New York: Harper-Collins, 1990), p. 46.

"Time is one loan
even a grateful recipient cannot repay."
Seneca

CHAPTER SIX

FATHERS: FOLLOW THE (ELUSIVE) LEADER

In the 1980s, baby boomers had reached the executive suites of America's corporations and their children had reached their teen years. And those fathers found in unprecedented numbers that there was a price to pay for success, and that price included time away from home. Guilt and problems soon followed.

In an *Fortune* magazine cover story entitled "Executive Guilt: Who's Taking Care of the Children?" author Fern Chapman revealed the findings of a survey commissioned by the magazine that showed the high degree of guilt that is associated with success in America's corporate boardrooms.[1] Nearly 30% of the men in the survey said that they had refused a new job, promotion, or transfer because it would have meant less family time. Sixty-one percent expressed concern that their children were being forced to conform to their parents' schedules, and 57% were concerned that children did not get enough attention.

Rosabeth Moss Kanter in *When Giants Learn to Dance* asked successful executives what their accomplishments had cost them. Their answers almost always included "gaining weight, getting a divorce, getting in trouble with the family."[2] Executives with young children were particularly susceptible to discontent. A national study by Opinion Research Corporation found that male managers under forty were the least satisfied of any group in the work force with the amount of time their jobs left them for family life.

Some respond by juggling work and family simultaneously. An AT&T study of employees with children under 18 years old found that nearly three-fourths them said they dealt with family issues at work. Forty-one percent had lost at least one day's work in the three months prior to the poll to care for family matters. In addition, 77% of women and 73% of men surveyed take time away from work *regularly* to attend to their children — making phone calls or ducking out for a long lunch to go to a school play.[3]

The big losers in the time squeeze are the children. Ironically, while most parents claim that their long hours are to provide support for their family, studies show that while they provide fiscal support, parents are often absent in providing emotional support for their children. The Family Research Council of Washington, D.C. reports that "total contact time" between parents and children has dropped 40% over the past twenty-five years.[4] Victor Fuchs, who studied parental time available to children for more than a quarter of a century, reports that in the average household, there are ten less hours of *potential* parental time per week — a figure that matches almost precisely with the figures of how much the work week has increased.[5] There is no doubt that the rise of long-hour jobs has come at the expense of family time. Over the last decade the length of the average family vacation has declined 14%, and the number of families that eat their evening meals together has dropped 10%.[6]

In one often-cited study, researchers found that the average child received only eight minutes of uninterrupted solo time with her father daily and only eleven minutes with her mother.[7] Christian author Josh McDowell, trying to replicate that study in Christian homes, found that the average time a church-attending father spent with his child was actually *lower*.[8] Interestingly, McDowell found a positive correlation between the teens who reported good communication with their fathers and those who were not yet sexually active. For a group of people who believe that we reap what we sow (Gal. 6:7), Christians seem to be doing very little "sowing" in terms of parenting, yet they naively hope to "reap" God-fearing children. Consequently, many evangelical groups report losses of up to 50% of the children reared in their churches.

Parents notice the problem, but their economic situations renders them virtually powerless to do anything about it. A national survey commissioned by the Massachusetts Mutual Insurance Company found that nearly half the parents who responded were concerned about not having enough time to spend with their families. The majority believed that "parents having less time to spend with their families" is the single most important reason for the decline of the family in American society.[9]

To soothe the guilt of this loss of contact time, parents turned to the concept of "quality time" with their children. In their 1987 book *Quality Parenting*, Linda Albert and Michael Popkin assured Moms and Dads that by working hard at the content and caliber of their interaction with their children, parents could transform ordinary moments into encounters that, like "a healthy diet high in natural foods and vitamins . . . sustains the kids throughout the day" when they had to be busy elsewhere.[10]

But "quality time" hasn't seemed to be the remedy to the problem. As Stephen Covey points out in *The 7 Habits of Highly Effective People*:

> You simply can't think *efficiency* with people. You think *effectiveness* with *people* and *efficiency* with *things*. . . I've tried to give ten minutes of "quality time" to a child or an employee to solve a problem, only to discover such "efficiency" creates new problems and seldom resolves the deepest concern.[11]

Deborah Fallows points out that quality time studies focus only on "all-out, undisturbed, down-on-the-floor-with-the-blocks time" and fail to provide an accurate gauge of parental influence on their children. Such methodologies, she says, discount the importance of *merely being together*.[12] In *When the Bough Breaks*, Sylvia Hewlett suggests that the drop in contact time reported in the studies above are significant because:

> many of the things parents do with children, whether it's visiting Grandma or shopping for groceries, play an important role in building strong parent-child relationships and giving families a shared identity.[13]

Quality time in the absence of a quantity of time has three flaws. First, relationships grow over time and cannot be rushed no matter how high the "quality" of the time is. Second, values are best learned when they are "caught" not "taught" and they can only be "caught" if children are spending sufficient time with their parents to observe them make the myriad of choices that together communicate those values to our children. Third, few people who espoused the idea of quality time realized the energy and originality that it would take. To fathers and mothers who invest long hours in their careers and come home at seven or eight o'clock, tired and preoccupied, the "magic bullet called quality time" was an appealing idea, says Hewlett. "The only problem is that most parents find it almost impossible to conjure up these sustaining encounters at the end of a stress-filled working day." [14]

In *Running Hard Just to Keep Up*, Sylvia Hewlett says that between 1973 and 1987, wages, after adjusting for inflation, fell by 19%. Given the fact that most American families were, by that time, trapped on the consumer treadmill of "work and spend," it is little surprise that the percentage of Americans who reported to pollsters that they were "very happy" peaked in 1957. And since work has played such an important part of the male psyche it is little wonder that as income fell the divorce rate doubled.[15] The proportion of a man's adult life spent living with a spouse and children now stands at 43% — the lowest in our history.[16]

Demographers Peter Uhlenberg and David Eggebeen calculate that the average number of years men aged twenty to forty-nine spend in families rearing children has dropped 40% in twenty years.[17] In simple terms, families aren't sticking together and men aren't sticking around to help rear the children they have fathered. This absence of males in the home meant that a child born in the late 1980s and early 1990s had an *80% chance* of growing up in a single parent household sometime in their first eighteen years.

Father absence is twice as common as it was a generation ago, and there is no relief on the horizon. Today, more than a quarter of all children are living without a father — some 10 million the product of marital separation and divorce and nearly 5 million the product of out-of-wedlock births.[18] Given those statistics, is it any wonder that a Michigan State University study showed that one child in three under the age of six would rather give up his daddy than his television?[19]

When fathers are absent from the home, drastic changes, most often for the worse, begin to occur. The income of ex-wives and their dependent children plummets after divorce. Women's standard of living drops, on average, 30% in the five years after divorce.[20] This immediate drop in available income leads to drastic changes in lifestyle for all but a few lucky victims of divorce. Most divorces kick off a cycle of long work hours for the custodial parent to provide even an approximation of their former lifestyle, meaning that children get shuffled from school to daycare or self-care.

The problems of absent fathers go far beyond economics. In *When the Bough Breaks*, Sylvia Hewlett contends that "a father's contribution to family life goes way beyond his paycheck."[21] That truth is illustrated by numerous studies which show that children that come from single parent homes are underachievers at school and more likely to be involved in trouble.

For instance, while some 10 to 15% of all teenage girls have some type of eating disorder[22] one study showed that 46% of those adolescents with eating disorders came from "chaotic families."[23] Laurel Mellin, director of the Center for Adolescent Obesity in San Francisco, sees these eating disorders as intimately linked to family dysfunction.[24]

> Mother's increasing presence in the work place, father's failure to pick up the residual fifty percent of parenting . . . and marital instability [all contribute to a situation where] children are not likely to receive the balance of warm nurturing support and effective limit setting that protects them from exhibiting various forms of distress, including eating and weight problems.

A study of 752 families by researchers at the New York Psychiatric Institute found that youngsters who attempted suicide did not differ from those who didn't in terms of age, income, race, and religion. However, they were *much more likely* "to live in non-intact family settings" and to have minimal contact with their fathers.[25]

A 1989 survey of teenagers discharged from psychiatric hospitals found that 84% were living in disrupted families when they were admitted.[26] According to a 1988 UCLA study, among homes with two parents and a "strict" father, only 18% of children used alcohol or drugs. In contrast, among single-mother homes, 35% of children used drugs frequently.[27]

The problems of single parent homes are manifest in the classroom as well. Thirty percent of all children with two parents were ranked as high achievers, compared to only 17% of one-parent children. Twenty-three percent of two-parent children were low achievers — while 38% of the one-parent children fell into this category."[28] A survey carried out by Columbia University and Bowling Green State University comparing the SAT scores of students from father-absent homes with those of students from father-present homes found that father absence had a "dramatic" negative effect on scores, a result that could not be explained away by differences in income.

Fathers are needed in the home. They're needed emotionally, economically, socially and spiritually. However, *effective* fathers are preferable to fathers in name only. The following suggestions are made in the hope of helping to make more effective fathers.

1. *Be a father, not just a manager*

Why is it that so many men who are successful in business are failures as fathers? Perhaps the answer is that the two enterprises are more vastly different than we ever imagined. In an article entitled "Why Grade 'A' Execs Get an 'F' as Parents," *Fortune* magazine warned in its January 1990 issue:

> Don't think that your brains, money or success will pave the way to parenting glory . . . the intensity and single-mindedness that make for corporate achievement are often the opposite of the qualities needed to be an effective parent."[29]

According to Susan Davies Bloom, a Connecticut family therapist, "professionals are so accustomed to functioning at a high level of control at the office that when they get home, they try to exert the same kind of control"[30] often with disastrous results.

2. *Be willing to sacrifice*

Sylvia Hewlett speaks of parenting as a sacrifice not all wish to make.[31]

> As we now understand, time and attention are at least as important as money in the child-raising enterprise. The fact

is parenthood involves a great deal of adult self-sacrifice. Children are no longer the economic assets they once were on the family farm. In the modern world raising a family is an extremely expensive proposition. But beyond these economic costs, responsible parenthood involves the expenditure of a great deal of energy and effort.

In an earlier age of agriculture and tradesmen, families were larger since children were an economic boon to the family. Children who could help with the chores while young and take over the enterprise when grown were a part of the economic security of the family. In today's urban culture, where few families own land or work in a self-employed trade, the situation is different. Today, children involve major expenditures of money with no financial return. Estimates of the cost of raising a child range from \$171,000 to \$265,000.[32] In return for such expenditures, "a child is expected to provide love, smiles and emotional satisfaction, but no money or labor," according to Viviana Zelizer in *Pricing the Priceless Child*. In the late Twentieth Century "a child is simply not expected to be useful" to his or her parents, she says.[33] Parenting today is a true sacrifice rather than the investment it once was and many are not making it.

Psychiatrist David Guttmann talks about the "routine, unexamined heroism of parenting." He claims that parents must "surrender their own claims to personal omnipotentiality" to their newborn child, something that many absent fathers have refused to do.[34] Good marriages and good parent-child relationships are expensive and the currency of choice is time. There are no shortcuts and everybody must pay.

3. *Keep yourself healthy*

In a 1992 survey conducted by the National Recreation and Park Association, 38% of all respondents said they "always felt rushed." One of the most significant findings, however, was that respondents who worked 15 minutes of exercise daily into their schedules were only half as likely to feel rushed as their non-exercising counterparts.[35]

In a survey for *Runner's World* magazine, the number one excuse runners made for not exercising was "not enough time in the day."[36] However, research shows that we can't afford to *not* exercise. Given the physical and mental benefits of daily exercise, time spent in exercise seems to return to the exerciser in more efficiency, fewer illnesses, better sleep patterns and a variety of other manifestations.

4. Consider "Downshifting"

A "downshifter" is defined as a person who voluntarily steps off the fast career track, opting for a slower, or in some cases, a regressive career track in exchange for more freedom. In *Downshifting*, Amy Saltzman identifies five types of persons who had left the fast track in exchange for a higher quality of lifestyle. She classifies them as:

> The *plateauer*, who finds a job within a comfortable zone of pay and responsibilities and chooses to stay there rather than accept promotions that come with relocations and higher time demands.

> The *back tracker*, who actually moves back down the career ladder in search of that niche that provides a comfortable level of income with a maximum amount of freedom.

> The *career shifter* who finds a less stressful career, often shifting from management to team member, or from owner to employee.

> The *self employee* who finds greater freedom in working for themselves. In a survey of some 3,000 new business owners, 54% said having "greater control over their life" was among the most important reasons for opening their own business. Thirty-two percent placed being able to "live where and how I like" at the top of their list.

The *urban escapee* who joins the growing number of individuals emigrating from large cities to do their work in areas more conducive to rearing children and relaxing. These are not commuters, they are residents of rural areas who either find employment in those communities or use technologies such as modems and fax machines to link to their work in metropolitan communities.

5. *Keep the family intact*

Fathers are needed in families and that is one reason, I believe, that God told his people through Malachi that he "hates" divorce (Mal. 2:16). In Matthew 5:31-32, Jesus refused to be trapped between the two warring schools of Jewish thought on the issue of divorce when he set adultery as the only acceptable cause for ending a marriage. Yet too many Christian marriages are ending based on the rationalization that "God wants me to be happy." In the wake of that poor excuse lie shattered children and spouses. Weldon McElreath, administrator of the largest denominational childcare facility in the United States, calls his charges "social orphans," children whose parents are living, yet who have been abandoned by them.[37]

Not all the problems of children today are the result of dysfunctional families or the busy schedules of parents. However, this generation of parents is failing in unprecedented numbers to stick together and the toll is showing in a variety of ways. As we noted earlier, absent fathers have been linked statistically with many problems faced by their children affected by the split including drug and alcohol abuse, suicide attempts, need for psychiatric care, low achievement in school, and eating disorders. The message is undeniable: children do better in intact family settings.

6. *Take the leadership role seriously*

For too long, Christians have used Ephesians 5:22-33 solely as a passage about authority patterns in the home, quoting only the fragment about wives submitting to their husbands. We need to re-examine what being a leader means. Paul says it means heading the home as Christ heads the church. For Jesus, His leadership meant the ultimate sacrifice: death. Twice in His ministry — early in the desert when Satan tempted Him and late in his life when He lay in the Garden of Gethsemane — Jesus could have taken an easier route. But He refused. And Paul commands that we lead our families like Christ led the church (Eph. 5:23) — never backing down from the challenges of leadership.

For instance, the participation of fathers is a key factor in whether children attend worship, according to author and lecturer Paul Faulkner. In his research, he found that children are nearly five times more likely to attend worship when both parents attend.[38]

In a recent speech, Senator Bill Bradley spoke of a book club offer his wife had received offering "No risks, no commitments." "Not a bad deal, but you can lose out on a lot in life by not taking risks or making commitments," Bradley remarked. Perhaps some fathers have yet to learn the difference between a family and a book club.

Endnotes

1. Fern Chapman, "Executive guilt: Who's taking care of the children?" *Fortune*, February, 1987, pp. 30-37.

2. Rosabeth Moss Kanter, *When Giants Learn to Dance* (New York: Simon & Schuster, 1989), p. 268.

3. Amy Saltzman, *Downshifting* (New York: HarperCollins, 1991), p. 34.

4. Sylvia Hewlett, "Running hard to keep up." *Time*, Fall, 1990.

5. Victor Fuchs, *Women's Quest for Economic Equality* (Cambridge, MA: Harvard University Press, 1986), p. 111.

6. Staff. "The Changing American Vacation," *Newsweek*, August 28, 1989, p. 8.

7. S.G. Timmer, J. Eccles, and K. O'Brien, "How children use their time." In F.G. Juster and F.P. Stafford (Eds.) *Time, goods and well-being* (Ann Arbor: University of Michigan Press, 1985), pp. 352-382.

8. Josh McDowell, "Study shows church kids not waiting." *Christianity Today*, March 18, 1988, pp. 54-55.

9. *Mass. Mutual Family Values Study.* Washington, DC: Mellman & Lazarus Inc., 1989.

10. Linda Albert and Michael Popkin, *Quality Parenting* (New York: Random House, 1987), p. 4.

11. Stephen Covey, *The 7 Habits of Highly Effective People* (New York: Simon and Schuster, 1989), pp. 169-170.

12. Deborah Fallows, "A Mother's Work" cited by Megan Rosenfeld in "Thanks a Bunch," *Washington Post*, November 9, 1986, Sec H, p. 3.

13. Sylvia Hewlett, *When the Bough Breaks* (New York: Basic Books, 1991), p. 73.

14. *Ibid.*, p. 84.

15. Sylvia Hewlett, "Running Hard Just to Keep Up." *Time*, Fall, 1990. Special Issue entitled *Women: The Road Ahead.*

16. Susan Watkins, Jane Menken, and John Bongaarts, "Demographic Foundations of Family Change," *American Sociological Review*, 52 (1987), pp. 346-358.

17. David Eggebeen, and Peter Uhlenberg, "Changes in the Organization of Men's Lives: 1960-1980." *Family Relations*, 34, (1985), p. 255.

18. *Studies in Marriage and the Family* (U.S. Bureau of the Census, Current Population Reports Series P-23, No. 162, 1989), p. 5.

19. Cited in Pete Hamil, "Crack and the box: Television helps pave the way to addiction." *Esquire*, May, 1990, pp. 66-69.

20. Lenore Weitzman, *The Divorce Revolution* (New York: The Free Press, 1985), p. 323.

21. Hewlett, *When the Bough Breaks*, p. 94.

22. Select Committee on Children, Youth and Families, *Eating Disorders: The Impact on Children and Families* (Washington, DC: U.S. House of Representatives, July 31, 1987), p. 3.

23. Hewlett, *When the Bough Breaks*, p. 71.

24. Testimony of Laurel M. Mellin, Director, Center for Adolescent Obesity, School of Medicine, University of California, San Francisco, before the Select Committee on Children, Youth and Families, in *Eating Disorders*, p. 19.

25. Carmen Noemi Velez and Patricia Cohen, "Suicidal Behavior and Ideation in a Community Sample of Children: Maternal and Youth Reports." *Journal of the American Academy of Child and Adolescent Psychiatry*, 27 (1988), pp. 349-356.

26. Helen S. Merskey and G.T. Swart, "Family Background and Physical Health of Adolescents Admitted to an inpatient Psychiatric Unit: 1, Principal Caregivers." *Canadian Journal of Psychiatry*, 34 (1989), pp. 79-83.

27. Robert H. Coombs and John Landsverk, "Parenting Styles and Substance Use During Childhood and Adolescence." *Journal of Marriage and the Family*, 50 (1988), pp. 473-482.

28. National Association of Elementary School Principals Staff Report "One-Parent Families and Their Children." *Principal*, 60 (September, 1980), pp. 31-37.

29. Brian O'Reilly, "Why Grade 'A' Execs Get an 'F' as Parents," *Fortune*, January 1, 1990, pp. 36-37.

30. *Ibid.*

31. Hewlett, *When the Bough Breaks*, p. 97.

32. Andrea Rock, "Can You Afford Your Kids?" *Money*, July, 1990, pp. 88-99.

33. Viviana A. Zelizer, *Pricing the Priceless Child* (New York: Basic Books, 1985), p. 3.

34. David Gutmann, *Reclaimed Powers: Toward a New Psychology of Men and Women in Later Life* (New York: Basic Books, 1987), p. 198.

35. Geoffrey Godbey and Alan Graffe, "Rapid Growth in Rushin' Americans." *American Demographics*, April, 1993, pp. 26-28.

36. Gordon Bloch, "I Don't Have Time." *Runner's World*, January, 1991, pp. 32-35.

37. Bill Marvel, "Little Orphan Annie would hardly recognize the place." The *Dallas Morning News*, November 28, 1991, Sec. C, pp. 1-2.

38. Paul Faulkner, "Getting ahead and taking your children with you." Public lecture in Oklahoma City, OK (December 8, 1991).

"Gather ye rosebuds while ye may,
Old Time is still aflying."
Robert Herrick

CHAPTER SEVEN

MOTHERS: WORKING A DOUBLE SHIFT

The titles beckon from the newsstand. "Create More Time," "Get Hip to Routines," says *Parents* magazine. "How to Add an Hour to your Day," says *Family Circle*. "Doing Too Much? Ten Sneaky Shortcuts," "Why Time Flies and How to Slow it Down," advises *McCalls*. "Scrambling for Time: Read This" urges *Working Woman*. But far from being the quick cures the titles imply, the overwhelming feeling many women feel when they read these titles is guilt: why does everyone else seem to have it together but me?

Until a little over a generation ago, women in the workforce were rare, mostly because the need was low. In the 1950s, a (usually male) worker's real earnings grew by 63%. In the next ten years, earnings increased 49%. As a result, getting ahead and standing out hardly required fathers to work 60 to 70 hours a week, and rarely required two incomes per family.[1] As the median wage climbed, America went on a unprecedented spending spree. Items once thought to be "luxuries" became staples in the American households. For instance, from 1983 to 1988, we bought 62 million microwave ovens, 57 million washers and dryers,

88 million cars and light trucks, 105 million color television sets, 46 million refrigerators and freezers, 63 million VCR's, 31 million cordless telephones and 30 million telephone answering machines. Debt accumulated, savings dwindled and still America kept buying.[2]

Then, quite suddenly, incomes started to drop. Suddenly, a 30-year old male during the 1980s was earning an average of *10% less* than his father did, adjusted for inflation. Items bought on the theory that wages would always go up were now a major drag on the budget.

The solution to this unexpected shortfall was found right at home in what researcher Arlie Hochschild calls an "artificially undervalued resource:" mom. Today more than half of all married women work outside the home and the number is rising. The presence of children in the home seems to be no factor in whether a mother works outside the home. More than two-thirds of the married women with children between the ages of six and seventeen work outside the home as do more than one-half of married women with children under six.

Here's how rapidly things have changed. In 1950 it was so rare for married women with children under the age of one to work outside the home that the Bureau of Labor kept no statistics on it. But today half of these mothers do.

For many, the move was hardly a voluntary one. One recent poll revealed that only 13% of the mothers responding wanted to work full time, although 52% of the respondents did so. Whether they wanted to work or were forced to work by economic circumstance, reality soon set in: the earning power of this new labor force was low. Several factors caused the low wages. First, ages-old notions of sexism entered in, paying women slightly more than half of men's wages even when they performed virtually the same task. Second, a substantial percentage of this new group of employees entered the labor force without higher education, settling for entry level jobs in the service sector. Third, because so many women wanted to work at once, market forces conspired to lower wages according to supply and demand.

Therefore, the desired relief on strained family budgets was slight. By 1988, the average family buying power after taxes was *only six percent higher* than in 1973, even though *twice as many* married women were working. In many households, layoffs and cutbacks meant that the two paltry paychecks didn't replace the one good income that was lost. Even in well-paying managerial jobs, women still earned only about 57% of what their male counterparts earned for the same positions in the early 1990s. For the lucky ones with good jobs, the reality of day care, additional taxes and the need for a sufficient wardrobe and reliable transportation to these new jobs meant that several homes had very little real increase to show for the new full-time worker in the family.

Even faced with the fact that mom's paycheck was not valued at what she was worth, and undaunted by the scarcity of quality day care, most families opted to continue the two-paycheck lifestyle. Today, two-job families are the norm for married couples with children. And few of the jobs are flexible. Of the mothers who work, 65% have jobs requiring thirty-five hours or more weekly.

Some families cope with small paychecks and expensive or non-existent day care by letting young children, often as young as preschool age, care for themselves. Children in such "self care" arrangements now number about seven million, and up to one-third of preschool children are thought to be left at home alone part of each day.[3]

Often the decisions of what to do with the children are made based on what is best for the adult and not the child. James Garbino, president of Chicago's Erikson Institute for Advanced Study in Child Development says:

> With infants, it's how soon they can go to day care so the parents can go to work? With 8- or 9-year-olds, it's how soon can they come home alone? It's all designed to make the participation of adults in the work force easier.[4]

David Elkind, a Tufts professor and authority on child development says of the young children we leave to go to work:

> We see children as competent even though there's no evidence that they are, because we need children who can handle day care, before-school programs, after-school programs, the things they see on TV. So we've revised our perceptions of childhood in line with our needs.[5]

However, some companies are getting innovative in their ways to help parents be two places at once. On-site day care is now common. Even sick children have a place to go. First Bank System of Minneapolis pays 75% of the daily cost for each employee's child who checks in to "Chicken Soup," a sick-child day care operation in Minneapolis. Maternal leave is now the law. However, women who attempt to take off extended periods of time may find that work follows them or stacks up. Author Amy Saltzman interviewed a woman who returned from a 4½ month maternity leave to find *15,000 electronic mail messages* awaiting her.

When women's roles changed outside the home, inside the home they remained the primary caregiver. This created a strain. Obviously, the more hours mothers are employed, the fewer hours they have available for "primary-care activities" such as playing with, talking to, dressing, feeding, and chauffeuring children and helping with homework. While the needs of children remain the same, "total contact time" between parents and children has dropped 40% during the last quarter-century. Mothers are stretched and few fathers have stepped into the breach to help.

University of Maryland sociologist John Robinson has the data that shows that employed mothers get few breaks when they get home. His research has shown that employed mothers spend an average of six hours each week in primary child-care activities — just under half the average time logged by nonemployed mothers but still roughly twice that of fathers. [6]

When mothers work outside the home, some of the traditional roles get contracted out. Other jobs go undone. In *The End of the American Century*, economist Steven Schlosstein tells us how the average Japanese mother visits her child's school twice a month, and every day "the child carries a notebook back and forth to school, in which mother and teacher alternately write notes regarding the child's health, mood and activities both at home and at school."[7] This is in stark contrast with the United States, where only a quarter of parents *ever* visit their child's school.

This is *not* an indictment of the mother who works outside the home. For many, it is an economic necessity. Regardless of the working arrangement of the family, who works and when they work pales compared to the major issue of keeping the family together. Children can adapt to a working mother much more readily than an absent father. Read *carefully* the quote below. In it, David Blankenhorn of the Institute for American Values claims that keeping families intact a part of the "moral agreement" we have with our children.

> The moral rule is that you do not bring a child into this world without a mother or father devoted to that child's well being. I'm not in favor of going back to the 1950s family, predicated on separate-sphere family roles with the woman playing the role of the lifelong homemaker. Roles can, and should, shift. But the number and identity of the parents in the household should remain the same.[8]

Just as women are the primary caregivers to the children in the family, they are also the primary cooks and house-cleaners as well. Studies show that most women are working two full-time jobs — employee and homemaker. In *The Second Shift*, Arlie Hochschild found that nearly all the women in her sample worked one shift at the office or factory and a "second shift" at home, straining them to their limit.

> Adding together the time it takes to do a paid job and to do housework and childcare . . . women worked roughly fifteen hours longer each week than men. Over a year, they worked an *extra month of twenty-four-hour days a year.*[9]

A 1985 study of 651 workers in a Boston-based corporation reveals the wide gap in total working hours between employed men and women. Of the employees studied, the married mother averaged working 85 hours a week on the job and at home. The married father averaged 66 hours – a nineteen-hour-per-week leisure gap. *All* of the studies I read showed a significant leisure gap between fathers and employed mothers and some studies have put the gap as high as 30 hours a week.

Hochschild claims that families have been hit by a "speed-up" in work and family life and that it is mainly women who have absorbed it. When women were pressed into the workforce, the same amount of housework remained to be done, but the available hours to do it lessened resulting in a "speed-up" just to get the same amount done.

Only twenty percent of the men in Hochschild's study shared housework equally. In an *American Demographics* article entitled "Who's Doing the Housework?" John Robinson found that 24% of employed wives do *all* of the housework and 42% of employed wives do *the bulk* of the housework.[10] But even when couples shared more or less equitably in the *amount* of work at home, they differed greatly in the *type* of work. Hochschild found that women did two-thirds of the routine, daily jobs at home, like cooking and cleaning up that fixed them into a rigid routine while men did many of the maintenance chores that could be postponed or done at convenient hours. Even children are of little help in the "second shift." A survey by the Massachusetts Mutual Life Insurance company in the summer of 1994 found that the average child reported having only two chores daily and spending only a few minutes on each chore.

Not surprisingly, the "second shift" takes its toll. In interviewing women for *The Second Shift,* Hochschild reported that

> Many women I interviewed could not tear away from the topic of sleep. They talked about how much they could "get by on" . . . six and a half, seven, seven and a half, less, more. They talked about who they knew who needed more or less. Some apologized for how much sleep they needed — "I'm afraid I need eight hours of sleep — as if eight was "too much."[11]

At the same time women were hit with the speed up of double duty, Madison Avenue was perpetuating the myth of "effortless perfection" in their commercials. Women who watched television saw other women who balanced family, stimulating careers and romance from early morning until late in the evening and yet their hairspray, pantyhose, deodorant or whatever never gave out. The unstated message of these ads is that if your life (or your products) are something less, then you are settling for too little.

With Madison Avenue constantly trying to define for us the "good life," the question of Zechariah becomes a pertinent one. He asked, "Who despises the day of small things?" (Zech. 4:10). In a day when most women are looked at as a wage earner, the primary care-giver for children and the primary employee of the "second shift" in the home, many days will have only "small things" to show for them. Our commercial messages may despise the ordinary things, such as the heroism of being a mother, but God doesn't and your family shouldn't. Here are some suggestions for balancing motherhood with your hectic pace of life.

1. *Rethink your work goals*

One recent survey found that more than a quarter of all women surveyed have given up a raise or promotion because it would have meant less family time. In a 1989 survey conducted by Robert Half International, Inc., 82% of the women surveyed said they would choose a career path with flexible full-time work hours and more family time, but slower career advancement, over one with inflexible work hours and faster career advancement. Two out of three said they would be willing to reduce their work hours and salaries (by an average of 13%) in order to have more family and personal time. Only one-third said they would be likely to accept a promotion if it required them to spend less time with their families.

2. *Place a priority on leisure*

In a 1990 poll by the Roper Organization, for the first time in fifteen years more respondents said "leisure" (41%), rather than "work" (36%), was "the most important thing" in their lives. Five years earlier, work had come out ahead of leisure by a score of 46% to 33%.[12]

Families need leisure activities to bind them together. David Blankenhorn has an exercise where he shows women a photo of a "perfect" 1950s family having a barbecue on the beach to test their attitudes about family. He reports that

> Members of the media and academic elites look at the photo and laugh. They say things like "That's what I've been fighting against all my life." But most other people look at it wistfully. One woman said, "I know the 'Ozzie and Harriet' stuff is impossible; but I miss the *familyness* of it."[13]

Leisure is not old-fashioned or out-of-date. Time spent together provides the experiences which bind families together. Book a time for leisure and keep it like any other appointment in your schedule. Leisure will not come by accident in our hurried and harried pace. It has to be planned and executed like any other part of our schedule.

3. *Learn the fine art of saying "no"*

In *Time Management for Christian Women*, authors Helen Young and Billie Silvey recommend that we confront our schedules with the advice we give small children, "Don't take such big bites." Daily we are tempted to bite off more than we can chew, and we do it, not because we want to but because we hate to say no.[14]

One of the first talks Linda, my wife, and I had after learning that she had multiple sclerosis was how she would have to cut back her substantial volunteerism schedule and her successful career as one of the nation's top decorative artists. Though she still does much of both, she does them in more measured quantities. The decisions were painful, but circumstances had dictated that she could no longer burn the candle at both ends. And so far, she says, she doesn't feel cheated by having to cut back.

Lord willing, you will not be forced by health considerations to make those kinds of decisions. But there is no reason why you should wait to be confronted with disabling illness or old age to learn to live a more measured life.

4. *Don't downplay small accomplishments*

One of the oldest adages of the stage is "There are no small parts, only small actors." Similarly, no part of a mother's day is small. Zechariah asked, "Who despises the day of small things?" Where children are involved, the answer to "What did you do today?" is never "Nothing."

It doesn't take an heroic effort to make an impact. In a 1989 survey 1,500 schoolchildren were asked, "What do you think makes a happy family?" The youngsters did not list money, cars, fine homes or televisions. Instead the number one answer was, "doing things together."[15] Similarly in a national survey commissioned by the

Massachusetts Mutual Insurance Company, pollsters found that nearly half the parents who responded were concerned about not having enough time to spend with their families. The majority believed that "parents having less time to spend with their families" is the single most important reason for the decline of the family in American society.[16] Children and parents agree: a little time is not a little thing. It can go a long way in binding a family together.

Endnotes

1. Amy Saltzman, *Downshifting* (New York: HarperCollins Publishers, 1991), p. 41.

2. Saltzman, p. 57.

3. John J. Sweeney and Karen Nussbaum, *Solutions for the Work Force* (Washington, DC: Seven Locks Press, 1989), p. 209.

4. Quoted in Jerry Adler, "Kids Growing Up Scared." *Newsweek*, January 10, 1994, p. 48.

5. Quoted in Adler, p. 47.

6. Cited in Sylvia Hewlett, *When the Bough Breaks* (New York: Basic Books, 1991).

7. Steven Schlosstein, *The End of the American Century* (Chicago: Congdon and Weed, 1989).

8. Joe Klein, "Whose Values?" *Newsweek*, June 8, 1992, p. 22.

9. Arlie Hochschild, *The Second Shift* (New York: Viking Press, 1989), p. 7.

10. John P. Robinson, "Who's Doing the Housework?" *American Demographics*, December, 1988, pp. 24-28.

11. Hochschild, *The Second Shift*, p. 9.

12. Cited in Saltzman, *Downshifting*, p. 17.

13. Klein, "Whose Values?" pp. 19.

14. Helen Young and Billie Silvey, *Time Management for Christian Women* (Nashville: Twenty-first Century Christian, 1990).

15. Nick Stinnett and John DeFrain, *Secrets of Strong Families* (Boston: Little, Brown, 1985), p. 81.

16. *Massachusetts Mutual Family Values Study* (Washington, DC: Mellman & Lazarus Inc., 1989).

*"Come to me,
all you who are weary and burdened,
and I will give you rest."*
Matthew 11:28

CHAPTER EIGHT

SPIRITUAL BURNOUT: WHAT TO DO WHEN THE FLAME DIES

Elijah was a man suffering a serious case of sudden "spiritual burnout," says Malcolm Smith in *Spiritual Burnout*. He hadn't slept in days. He was tired and hungry and ready to give up. Under a broom tree in the desert he sat down and prayed to God to end it all. "I have had enough, Lord," he said. "Take my life; I am no better than my ancestors" (1 Kings 19:4). With that request made, he slept, hoping that God would grant his request.

How did he get so low? He had just scored two tremendous spiritual victories. First, he had defeated 450 prophets of Baal by calling on God to bring fire from heaven onto his altar of twelve stones and consume his sacrifice, after the prophets of Baal had been unable to get fire from their god. After the victory, he had personally supervised the slaughter of all the false prophets. Second, he had fervently prayed to God and helped bring the end of a three-year drought to the land.

But now he was feeling anything but victorious as he fled into the desert. Queen Jezebel in her rage had vowed that Elijah would be dead within 24 hours. He ran at least a day's journey into the hot desert and fell when he could run no more, calling on God to take his life before Jezebel could do the job.

His sleep was brief. An angel awakened him and instructed him to eat and drink food divinely prepared for him. He ate and laid down again. Again he was awakened, this time with the instruction to "Get up and eat, for the journey is too much for you" (1 Kings 19:7). And on the strength of that food, he traveled for forty days to Horeb, the "mountain of God" near the place where God had given the law to Moses. There he found a cave and slept again.

The question that awakened him from that second slumber should awaken all of us from our daily rush as well. The Lord came to him and asked: "What are you doing here, Elijah?" (1 Kings 19:9). Of course, God didn't need to know why Elijah was there. He wanted Elijah to recognize where he was and how he got there. It's similar to the question God asked of Adam in Genesis 3:9 when he asked "Where are you?" God didn't need help in finding Adam's location. Adam needed help in pondering how his actions had gotten him there.

"Where are you?" "What are you doing here?" They're questions every father should ask himself when he works through a family supper. They're questions every mother should ask as she runs the shuttle between one urgent appointment and another. Elijah replied "I am the only one left and now they are trying to kill me too" (1 Kings 19:10). In saying this, Elijah was voicing a complaint that most of us who attempt to follow God feel at some point: "I've kept my end of the bargain, but has anybody else kept theirs?"

Two of Elijah's statements to God — "take my life" (1 Kings 19:14) and "I am the only one left" (1 Kings 19:14) — reflect what Malcolm Smith calls the "irrationality of the burned-out person."[1] If he had wanted to die, he need only have stayed close enough to Jezebel to get his "wish." And he wasn't the only one, either. Seven thousand faithful remained in Israel, a number so large it would have been impossible for Elijah not to have known that a faithful remnant remained. But individuals experiencing burnout aren't thinking about the rationality of their statements or their actions. And they will often stay in this irrational state until something or someone brings them out.

For Elijah, God passed a series of powerful natural phenomena in front of the cave to get his attention focused off himself. First came a wind so powerful it tore the mountains apart. Then came an earthquake and a fire. But God was nowhere to be found in these manifestations of power. Only when Elijah heard a gentle whisper did he find God.

Elijah's problem and his ultimate restoration is summed up this way by Smith:

> Secretly we all want God to be the Infinite Bully, to throw His power around and make people respect Him — and us. But when He throws his weight around, it is the weight of His love and grace. . . A person is healed of burnout when he receives a fresh revelation of Who God is. This does not make sense to human reasoning. . . The answer to spiritual burnout is to respond to God afresh, and discover a new relationship with Him.[2]

Elijah is not alone among the characters of the scriptures in his struggling with despair. Job's wife gave up. David interspersed laments of despair among his psalms of praise and thanksgiving. Jonah went the wrong way. Habakkuk questioned why God would punish the merely evil with the really evil. Peter denied Christ. Some of the apostles returned to fishing following the death of their Lord.

Jesus, in the parable of the soils, predicted that some followers would spring up in the Word but quickly die out. Perhaps that's why finishing the race is such an important metaphor to Paul. In 1 Corinthians 9:24-27 he gives the impression of a man who will not be denied the prize that lays before him when he reminds the Corinthians:

> Do you not know that in a race all the runners run, but only one gets the prize? Everyone who competes in the

games goes into strict training. They do it to get a crown that will not last; but we do it to get a crown that will last forever. Therefore I do not run like a man running aimlessly; I do not fight like a man beating the air. No, I beat my body and make it my slave so that after I have preached to others, I myself will not be disqualified for the prize.

I live in a suburban community where Olympic medalist Shannon Miller and a handful of other young girls live and train in hopes of representing the United States in international gymnastics competition. These young ladies give up practically all normalcy in their pursuit of gymnastic excellence. Many live apart from their parents to be near their coach. They have special arrangements for school. They have little social life outside of the gym where they often spend six hours daily.

Injury is not the main problem that threatens these young athletic careers. Shannon Miller competed in the 1992 Olympics about a month after wrist surgery. The major career threat is burnout — the possibility that the goal will someday not seem worth the sacrifice. That's when the athlete quits. That's when the Christian quits. That's when Elijah quit.

James makes the interesting statement in his epistle: "Elijah was a man just like us" (James 5:17). We all have the potential in us, like Elijah, to do something great for the Lord. Yet we also have the potential in us to get discouraged and quit as Elijah tried to do. In the hopes that you will finish your race, here are some suggestions for avoiding spiritual burnout.

1. *Refill the reservoir*

Why did God rest at the end of creation? Is it possible that the one who created the world and the heavens could tire? Undoubtedly not. His rest was to establish a precedent for us. Smith points out that our spiritual being can become ill if we abuse our physical bodies.

In dealing with the problem of spiritual burnout and exhaustion, we must not forget that we are spirits who live in physical bodies. And the resurrection of the body has not yet taken place! If we abuse our bodies, through the food we eat, lack of sleep, an overloaded schedule, little or no time to rest and recreate, we can be sure that it will be reflected in our frayed emotions, dull minds and weary spirits. In His love and wisdom, God was giving Elijah an emergency Sabbath rest, something that even fallen man was commanded to enjoy![3]

2. *Don't confuse boredom with burnout*

Because of the pace of our lives, it is possible to regard the routine, ordinary pace of life as boring. Bertrand Russell once remarked that "at least half of the sins of mankind" are caused by the fear of boredom. In his *Christianity Today* article, "Anything but Boredom!" author Donald McCullough suggests that the most promising strategy for dealing with boredom is to accept it as "an inevitable consequence of being made for more than life has to offer." He continues:

> Rather that running from it and seeking relief in all sorts of diversions, we ought to embrace it, open ourselves to it. . . [Boredom] forces us to see the ultimate emptiness of life in this world; it enables us to let go of diversions that distract us from being attentive to the presence of the Holy.[4]

Interestingly, the major time problem in the world is a surplus of time with little meaningful activity to fill it. Only in America and a handful of industrialized nations do we continually run into a scarcity of time. Consequently, when we are occasionally faced with little to do, we don't know what to do. The problem is especially acute with our children. They have been reared without the traditional "sit and wait" pace of childhood. Indeed, much of parenting in the 1990s is getting the kids to their myriad of activities. One child I know has no afternoons at home in her room at all.

She often has two or more lessons — pottery, dance, riding, band — in a single day. Her pace and the pace of other children like her is far from boring, but consequently it leaves them little time to imagine or reflect. Rather than despising or avoiding boredom, we should embrace it for what it is: calm between the storms of life and a reminder that better things are ahead for the Christian.

3. *Don't take your eyes off the prize*

The account of Peter walking on the water is an interesting one to me. The scriptures tell us that he joined Jesus on the water, "But when he saw the wind, he was afraid" (Matt. 14:30) and he began to sink. As long as his eyes were on Jesus, he was able to walk on the water. When he stopped to consider the plausibility of the situation, he looked down and sank. We can do marvelous things with our eyes on Jesus. It's when we take my eyes off Him that we begin to falter and sink.

Just because we are doing "good works" does not necessarily mean that our eyes are on the prize. Diane Fassel relates that in her seminars on workaholism, she finds the most resistance to her message from the ministers, including one who blurted out, "It's not OK to kill myself for work but it is OK to kill myself for Christ."[5]

4. *Don't put undue pressure on yourself*

William Sidis was a child prodigy. By the age of five, he could speak five languages. He could read Plato in the original Greek at an age when most children were preparing for kindergarten. He passed the admissions test to Harvard at age eight, but had to wait three years to be admitted. He graduated *cum laude* in 1914, a media darling through his frequent appearances in "Ripley's Believe It or Not" and nineteen front page mentions in the *New York Times*.

But by the time the *New Yorker* caught up with him in 1937 he was a recluse, having held a series of low-paying jobs and living in a seedy apartment strewn with the subway tokens he collected. He died in 1944 at the age of 46, leaving behind no major works or legacy.

What happened? Many psychologists have attempted to explain the early genius and later disappointment of Sidis. Perhaps he was not sufficiently psychologically developed to handle his mental prowess. The rest of his makeup was simply not up to the task of fame and expectation. Perhaps Sidis would have thrived without the media attention. Perhaps he would have been a more successful adult if he had enjoyed a more normal childhood.

No one knows for sure what might have caused Sidis to be a failure in life. But what is not in doubt is that Christians are susceptible to the same phenomenon as Sidis: an inability to live up to expectations. In Philippians 3:12-14 Paul says,

> Not that I have already obtained all this, or have been made perfect, but I press on to take hold of that for which Christ Jesus took hold of me. Brothers, I do not consider myself yet to have taken hold of it. But one thing I do: Forgetting what is behind and straining toward what is ahead, I press on toward the goal to win the prize for which God has called me heavenward in Christ Jesus.

This passage holds a key to avoiding spiritual burnout: don't ever expect to have it all together. Paul says he didn't, but he pressed on anyway and so should we.

When Paul wrote Timothy, he reminded him of his rich spiritual heritage that began with his grandmother, Lois, and continued through his mother, Eunice. But Paul didn't use this fact to lay a guilt trip on Timothy about what such a good head start should mean in terms of missionary output. Instead, he put the timing for Timothy's maturing right back into Timothy's hands when he said "For this reason (referring back to his heritage of faith) I remind you to fan into flame the gift of God" (2 Tim. 1:6).

The gift that God gave each of us is a delicate flame. Fail to feed it, and it will flicker out. Fuel it with every ounce of energy we have and we will burn out. Somewhere in between is the delicate balance. Check out God's gifts in 1 Corinthians 12 and 14. Find out what you can do for the kingdom then fan the flame, without undue pressure, and watch it grow.

Endnotes

1. Malcolm Smith, *Spiritual Burnout* (Tulsa: Honor Books, 1988), p. 160.

2. *Ibid.*, pp. 168-169.

3. *Ibid.*, p. 162.

4. Donald W. McCullough, "Anything but Boredom!" *Christianity Today*, August 19, 1991, pp. 30-32.

5. Diane Fassel, *Working Ourselves to Death* (San Francisco: HarperCollins, 1990), p. 116.

CHAPTER NINE

PREPARING TO MEET THE "GIANT"

From the day he was born, the Boy Who Would be King had a date with a giant.

Though he didn't know it at the time, as the small boy played with his sling in the woods, he was preparing for his date with the giant. As he got better, sending one smooth stone after another into his target, he was gaining the skill to fight the giant. And as the boy shepherd stayed with the sheep at night, protecting them from the occasional lion or tiger, he was gaining the courage to face the giant. Looking up at the stars while tending his flocks at night and seeing nature declare the existence of God, he was gaining the inner faith to beat the giant.

So when the time came for David the shepherd, the youngest son of Jesse, to battle the giant Goliath, he had been preparing his whole life for the day. His skills and his faith had come together for this special day.

From the day she was born, the Girl Who Would be Queen had a date with fate.

As a little girl, she could hear the admiring remarks of those around her. Phrases like "goddess" or "angel" were often used by those who came in contact with her stunning beauty for the first time. Some even said she was regal enough to be a queen.

As she grew, all around her were the teachings of a devout Jewish home: lessons of a God who had delivered his people in the past, and of a God who would deliver his people again. And as she grew, so too grew her string of admirers. One day she caught the eye of the emissary of the king who added her to the pool of women from which a new queen would be chosen.

It was in the palace that Esther, the beautiful young girl now grown, had her date with fate. Her people were set to be slaughtered, yet they could be saved by an edict of the king. But Esther could only go in to plead their case before him by invitation. To do otherwise was to risk death for displeasing the king. Reminded by her uncle that she might have been placed in the palace for "such a time as this" (Esther 4:14) Esther risked her life by entering into the presence of the king on behalf of her people. And what was to have been a slaughter of her people became a glorious victory instead.

David and Esther are but two examples of God using ordinary, willing people for his extraordinary purposes in the Old Testament. Yet, they did not suddenly find the courage and the skills needed at their moment in history. Instead, they were ready for their moment thanks to a lifetime of preparation. And in both cases, Jewish history was changed as a result.

About a decade ago, a new word became commonly used in the risk assessment business, those people in government and industry who make a living trying to predict, analyze and lower risk for the rest of us. Now you see it everywhere. The word is "proactive." It is the opposite of reactive and means to act beforehand. To be proactive is to see consequences before they occur and act before they can happen.

The proactive person or institution seeks to change outcomes by changing factors that would otherwise cause them. On a broad level, government programs such as Head Start, for instance, are justified as being proactive approaches to crime, poverty, illiteracy and the like. On an individual level, a proactive driver stays out of situations that might cause accidents. A proactive parent is interested in their child's total environment — school, friends, media, etc., trying to prevent the effects of bad influences before those influences can even occur.

The concept of proactivity is so important to a success-ful life that Stephen Covey, in *The 7 Habits of Highly Effective People*, lists "Be Proactive" as the first habit on which the others rest.[1] The more "proactivity" one does, the less "reactivity" is required at the last moment or after the fact. Think of how little adjustment two boats on a lake have to make to avoid a collision when they are 400 yards apart. Now place those boats 40 feet apart. That's the differ-ence in proaction and reaction.

Now here is the application. *Each of us has a giant in our future and what we do today could determine how we fare later.* For some the giant will be bad health, for others it will be a financial reversal or layoff. Some will have to take care of aging parents, others will be chal-lenged by rebellious teens. Some will join the one in eight Americans who have been divorced, others will experience the death of a spouse.

Since there is a challenge in your future, as large and as sure as those faced by David and Esther, the question becomes: how are you preparing? What have you done lately for that time when you will be tried? Will we do noth-ing and let it take us by surprise or will we be prepared and tackle the problem head on?

The scriptures endorse living in a proactive manner. Jesus taught it in the parable of the bridegroom and the ten bridesmaids in Matthew 25. The proactive ones had planned ahead for the crisis of no oil, the reactive ones let the crisis take them by surprise. Much of the stress, worry, pace and expense of life comes from our natural tendency to be reactive rather than proactive. We either don't see or don't think the bridegroom (or giant) is coming. And when he does we're not prepared.

The story is told of a farmer who needed to hire a ranch hand. The hand would be the only other worker on the farm, and the duties carried much responsibility. But like so many farm jobs, it paid little. So after a nearly futile search, the farmer interviewed the sole applicant for the job, he asked the young man what he felt was his main strength.

"I can sleep well on a stormy night," came the reply.

Having no other applicants and having a farm full of work to be done, the owner hired the curious young man and he proved to be a good worker. Day after day he performed the urgent chores and always found time for important chores as well.

Eventually, after an afternoon of threatening weather, a stormy night arrived with fury. The owner dashed from place to place on the farm finding everything secure and out of the weather. He also found his helper sound asleep in his small house. His wise use of time had prepared him to sleep through the storm.

There is an old Scottish axiom that goes "Thatch your roof while it is yet warm." In other words, prepare today for the storms of tomorrow. Here's an interesting thought: you don't have to know what storms are ahead to be able to sleep through them when they arrive. Because regardless of the nature of the storm, the answer will always be found in the strength of our faith and God's grace to deliver. The Christian, of all people, should be a proactive person. We not only know that storms will come, but having read the end of the book, we know who comes out victorious in the storms of life.

Towards the end of his trials, Job compared his experience to having been refined by fire. The analogy is from the silversmith trade. The refiner of the silver would heat the metal boiling hot to remove the imperfections so that only silver remained. At the right temperature the liquid metal would reflect the face of the refiner as he looked into it. So it was with Job's experience. At the time when the trials of his temptation boiled the hottest, Job still reflected the image of God.

It has been said that crises pull back the curtains we put up in our lives and bare the "backstages" of our soul. Job did not become a righteous man on the day that calamity struck him. He was a righteous man long before that; the calamity merely let his strong faith in God show through. Similarly, and sadly, the calamity was an opportunity for the weak faith of Job's wife to be revealed.

The old saying that "heroes are made, not born" is only partially accurate. While it is true that no one is genetically predisposed to be a hero, it does not follow that a hero can be "made" like one would attempt to make a star athlete or renowned musician through practice and hard work. A better truism would be that "heroes are revealed, not born." Crises reveal who is made of hero material.

Lenny Skutnik was revealed to be a hero on January 13, 1982. On that day, the 28-year old government employee plunged into the icy waters of the Potomac River to rescue one of the survivors of an Air Florida plane that had crashed near downtown Washington, D.C. in a blinding snowstorm. Others stood and watched. One man jumped in, but turned back in the numbing cold. Meanwhile, a flight attendant, Kelly Duncan, lost her grip on the helicopter rope and began to sink. Lenny Skutnik acted.

What did young Lenny or teen-aged Lenny do that readied him for that moment? We don't know and won't since he never talked about his heroism with the media who wanted to make a star of him. But when opportunity came to reveal who was the hero on the banks of the Potomac, it was Lenny Skutnik who stepped forward.

The Christian life calls for quiet heroes to step forward and slay giants. It will seldom make headlines, but the quiet heroism of parenting, being a spouse, being a care giver to an aging parent is heroism nonetheless. This type of heroism is a combination of opportunity, predisposition and preparation. If all of the three aren't present, the giant will win. When all three are in place, we can't fail as Paul reminds the Philippians: "I can do everything through him who gives me strength" (Phil. 4:13).

Given the fact that some "giant" is in my future, calling for me to be a hero, it is only natural to face the future with a certain measure of worry. Worry is so ingrained in our society that few Christians have stopped to consider that worry, as defined by Jesus in Luke 12, is both futile and faithless. Simply put, worry is sin.

However, we must properly differentiate worry from concern. Concern is a normal part of life. As a parent, I'm concerned when my teenaged daughter is out at night. I'm also concerned about my parents' health, the welfare of my former students, the wisdom of my congregation's elders and a multitude of other things.

However, when our normal, and Biblical, concern becomes all-consuming, we cross over the line into worry. In Luke 12:22-31, Jesus points out that worry is not a part of the plant or animal kingdom, and it should not be a part of the kingdom of God. Jesus says,

> Therefore I tell you, do not worry about your life, what you will eat; or about your body, what you will wear. Life is more than food, and the body more than clothes. Consider the ravens: They do not sow or reap, they have no storeroom or barn; yet God feeds them. And how much more valuable you are than birds! Who of you by worrying can add a single hour to his life? Since you cannot do this very little thing, why do you worry about the rest?
>
> Consider how the lilies grow. They do not labor or spin. Yet I tell you, not even Solomon in all his splendor was dressed like one of these. If that is how God clothes the grass of the field, which is here today, and tomorrow is thrown into the fire, how much more will he clothe you, O you of little faith! And do not set your heart on what you

eat or drink; do not worry about it. For the pagan world runs after such things, and your Father knows that you need them. But seek first his kingdom, and these things will be given to you as well.

Worry has no power. It can't add an hour to my life or an inch to your height. The list of things that worry *can't* do is endless: it can't grow hair, prevent wrinkles, balance a checkbook, etc., etc. If worry doesn't help with the small things of life, it's certain that it won't solve the major crises.

That passage in Luke 12 hit home to my family in 1993 when my wife, Linda, was diagnosed with multiple sclerosis. MS is a sometimes degenerative disease that has a multitude of manifestations (hence the name *multiple* sclerosis) that vary by individual. In Linda's case, the disease has twice taken the sight in her right eye for a month at a time. For an artist, a "taxi driver," and busy volunteer, this manifestation was particularly cruel and led to many anxious nights as we wondered if her sight would return.

Even when she has her full sight, which is most of the time, Linda now has to hold all objects with both hands as she is losing her ability to grasp. She also tires more quickly than before and has to say "no" now to some requests, a situation that she regrets. She hates to use "I'm tired" as a reason, saying it makes her feel "lazy."

Because of the nature of the disease, we don't know which additional symptoms she will contract (if any) or how severe they will be. For some, the disease is crippling, for others it is not. For some it lowers life expectancy about fifteen percent. My wife might (or might not) be one of those. We don't know. But one thing we are beginning to learn is that we will not add an hour to her life by worrying about it.

Some problems are present to make us more dependent on God. Why didn't God take away the "thorn in the flesh" that Paul complained of? One traditional answer is that the presence of the problem made Paul more dependent on

God. I like that answer. But I am also intrigued by the possibility that the infirmity could have been a physical limitation that forced Paul to work at a slower pace than he wished, giving him more time to reflect and to write. Perhaps its removal might have made him an entirely different apostle and correspondent to the churches. Maybe some infirmities are present to let other strengths flourish.

Are we concerned about my wife's health? Of course. Are we worried? Oddly enough, not really. By refusing to be consumed by the diagnosis, my wife has bravely demonstrated to me and to our three children that worry has no grip on the Christian. With her courage, we have stayed on the right side of the fine line between concern and worry. I wish I could tell you that I'm there in every aspect of my life, but I'm not.

There's an old sign that cropped up in several businesses a few years ago. It goes:

There two rules here.
1. Don't sweat the small stuff.
2. Everything is small stuff.

I still worry, and often I worry a lot. And in the words of the sign above, much of it falls in the realm of "the small stuff." And as I talk to other Christians, this seems to be a problem with many.

Our problem with distinguishing the "small stuff" is that nothing looks small when we are in the midst of it. All problems loom large when viewed from within. To get a better perspective, consider the interviews you read occasionally given by the elderly. Looking back, most express the sentiment that they wish they had worked less and played more. Many express a little remorse over opportunities lost to be a better parent, spouse or child. But you never see an interview with an elderly person where they express a desire to have worried more. As the perspective of life gets focused through the lens of experience, very little seems to warrant the emotional and physical damage that worrying causes.

One of two reasons usually lies at the root of most worries. First, there are worries that are present because there are some things in our lives that need fixing. If you worry about an IRS audit, perhaps you need to change the way you do your taxes. If you worry about dying, perhaps you need to change the way you are living.

Second, there are the worries that are present because of a lack of faith in the promises of God. God has promised us better treatment than the birds of the air or the grass of the field, and both seem perennially hardy each year. Won't he get us through family problems, job insecurities, poor health and the like?

When anxiety hits ask yourself these questions:

1. Is the worry caused by sin in my own life? Will it go away if I do something or quit doing something I am currently doing? If so, am I willing to take the steps necessary to stop the worry?
2. Is the worry caused by a lack of faith on my part in God's promises? Am I spending hours worrying about things that are basically out of my control and not essential in the eternal scheme of things?

Finally, follow the command of James 5:13 where we are reminded "Is any of you in trouble? He should pray." David meditated in the pastures before he faced his giant. Esther fasted in her room before she faced the king. Once you identify the source of the worry, and deliver it to God in prayer, you're on the way to remedying the problem.

Endnote

1. Stephen Covey, *The 7 Habits of Highly Effective People* (New York: Simon and Schuster, 1989).

"Be still, and know
that I am God."
Psalms 46:10

CHAPTER TEN

LISTENING TO THE TICKING OF OUR INTERNAL CLOCKS

For centuries, the only clocks were biological clocks that told humans when to rise, when to eat and when to sleep. When the psalmist proclaimed that we are "fearfully and wonderfully made," (Ps. 139:14) the internal regulators of the body were at least a part of the justification of that statement. After timepieces began to replace the biological clock in importance, it was centuries before science returned to take a serious look at the intricacy of the clock that is built within each of us. As scientists are beginning to probe the mysterious world of biological clocks, we are learning how perfectly matched our biological rhythms are with the tempo of the world around us and how that delicate balance can be destroyed by our work and/or play habits.

Jeremy Rifkin claims in *Time Wars* that the number of tasks that need to be choreographed within the human body is "awesome."[1]

Blood pressure, heartbeat, body temperature, metabolic rates, hormonal secretions, wake and sleep cycles, are only a few of the systems that need to be timed and coordinated with precision if the human body is to function properly. We have uncovered only a fraction of the many rhythms that permeate the physiology of the human organism. The kidneys function in tandem with the daily revolution of the earth. The liver processes its glycogen reserves according to a dependable circadian rhythm. Our body temperature also rises and falls in a predictable pattern every twenty-four hours. So, too, does our skin temperature.

These daily cycles, known as "circadian" (Latin for "about a day") cycles are but one of several timed cycles of the body. While most of our most basic internal processes follow a twenty-four-hour cycle, some of our biological clocks are attuned to lunar cycles, seasons or annual cycles. The cycles are even subject to change. Research shows sometime after a person reaches their mid-fifties, there is a shift in the length of some of the internal rhythms. This resetting of the internal clock, which occurs fairly rapidly, explains why more mature people go to sleep earlier, and wake up earlier.

Discovering the key to our circadian rhythms holds much promise for medical science. Researcher William Hrushesky has been exploring a relationship between cancer remission and administering the chemotherapy at certain key times during the day.[2] Anger and anxiety are but two of the emotions that can vary considerably during the day since both emotions require extra doses of adrenaline, a chemical available at different levels at different points of the day. Other events seem geared to a daily cycle. More births and deaths occur in the early morning hours than any other time. More heart attacks and strokes occur around nine a.m. than at any other hour.

Our annual clocks sometimes enter the physical and emotional picture as well. The peak number of deaths from heart disease occurs in January. The well-documented phenomenon of depression brought on by light deprivation during the shortest months of the year has a biological basis.

During the shorter days, the brain secretes more melatonin, which brings on depression. As the days lengthen, the pineal glands secrete less melatonin, alleviating the symptoms of depression brought on by the hormone.

Depression from light deprivation is quite real. One well-known youth minister told me he could hardly function in the month of February. My wife also suffered from it for years. My wife's solution to anticipate the problem by making a note on her calendar to watch for the symptoms of light deprivation depression in January and February and take steps to "reward herself with light" as she put it. For severely depressed patients, doctors are now recommending that they combat the problem by exposure to massive doses of artificial light which lowers the secretion of melatonin.

As our lives have sped up, Americans are showing symptoms of what has come to be known as "hurry sickness." Hurry sickness, according to internist Larry Dossey is "the belief that everything from sharpening a pencil to firing an employee must be done faster, faster, faster."[3] One manifestation of the disease is a distortion in one's sense of time. In his research, Dossey would ask a patient to sit quietly in a chair until he thought a minute had elapsed. Most patients were significantly under, including one man who said "That's a minute" nine seconds into the experiment. According to Dossey, far from being some harmless psychological quirk, such a speed-up in the mind is matched by a speed-up of bodily functions which hasten sickness and even death.

Probably our chief abuse of the body's natural rhythms is the manner in which the average American approaches sleep. Reporter Natalie Angier interviewed experts in sleep and sleep disorders for a 1990 report in the *New York Times* entitled "Cheating on Sleep." She reports that a majority of Americans are sleeping at least an hour to 90 minutes less each night than they should. We have become, she says, "the land of the drowsy."[4]

Few people realize that they are cheating themselves out of needed rest each night and even fewer are able to do anything about the cycle. "People cheat on their sleep, and they don't even realize they're doing it," Howard P. Roffwarg, director of the Sleep Study Unit at the University of Texas Southwestern Medical School in Dallas told Angier. "They think they're O.K. because they can get by on six and a half hours, when they really need seven and a half, eight or even more to feel ideally vigorous."[5]

"In our society, it's considered dynamic, a feather in one's cap, to say you only need five and a half hours sleep," as one sleep researcher told the *Times*. "If you say you've got to get eight and a half hours, people look at you askance, as though you lack drive and ambition."[6] As the complexity of our lives increases, many people simply consider sleep to be the most expendable item on the agenda.

"I can't think of a single study that hasn't found people getting less sleep than they ought to," added Dr. David F. Dinges, a biological psychologist at the Institute of Pennsylvania Hospital in Philadelphia. "Whenever I ask an audience how many people woke up by an alarm clock that morning, about two-thirds raise their hand," he said. "If that's how you wake up every day, you're shortening your natural sleep pattern."[7]

While research has shown that little has changed in a person's need to spend about a third of his or her life at rest, society seems to conspire against those who try to get adequate rest. We hear of corporate executives, politicians and other successful individuals who climb to the top on four to five hours of rest per night, and we embrace that as a route to success, rather than the life-shortening lifestyle that research indicates it is.

Society's cost for lost sleep is now beginning to be calculated. For instance, studies have shown that traffic accidents increase significantly the week after the clocks are changed in or out of daylight savings time. Similarly a study done on the trucking industry found that the chance of an accident increases by 200 percent at 5:00 a.m. Industry analysts are beginning to assess effect of shift work on the desynchronization of their biological clocks. Shift workers — about 22 percent of all employees, according to the Bureau of Labor Statistics — can suffer up to a net loss of one night of sleep per week. Shift workers' susceptibility to peptic ulcers and other stomach disorders is two to three times greater than the general population's. Their productivity is also significantly lower. According to several studies, Rifkin notes that worker error peaks between 3:00 a.m. and 5:00 a.m.[8]

The ramifications in the workplace are enormous as sleep deprived workers are more prone to making mistakes on the job. Though perhaps coincidental, it is important to note that the major industrial accidents at Three Mile Island (USA), Chernobyl (Russia), and Bhopal (India) all occurred at night, possibly because workers who monitor the equipment were not optimally alert. The Three Mile Island accident in particular might have been related to a desynchronization of the biological clocks of the night shift employees. The accident occurred at four in the morning and employees in charge of the facility at the time of the accident had been rotating shifts around the clock every week for a month and a half.

If America is indeed becoming the "land of the drowsy," the toll is quite high. At least 40,000 traffic accidents a year may be sleep-related, and *more than twenty percent* of all drivers report that they have fallen asleep at the wheel at least once. Higher rates of employee absenteeism due to illness toward the end of the week, once thought to be a form of "playing hooky" may actually be sleep related. Common sense dictates that a person who chronically sleeps ninety minutes less per night during the workweek than is necessary will feel worse on Friday than on Tuesday. "By the fifth night, you've lost seven and a half hours, or virtually a whole night's sleep," reports Dr. Dinges.[9] The result is higher employee absenteeism or lower productivity out of the ones who are at work.

However, even the experts don't always heed their own advice, Angier found. When asked about his sleep habits, one researcher replied "I get by on maybe six, six and a half hours. I'm just too busy to get a good night's sleep."[10]

At the same time that Americans are squeezing a night a week out of their optimum sleeping pattern, they are stuffing an extra half-day's work into their weekly schedules. In *The Overworked American*, Juliet Schor reports that U.S. blue collar workers put in 320 more hours per year than their counterparts in Germany or France[11] without counting overtime. White collar professionals squeeze in an extra month of work per year by working overtime, taking working lunches, ignoring vacations and taking work home.[12]

While the major time problem in most of the third world is too much time and too little to do, Americans have just the opposite problem: too much to do and too little time. And the only two ways to create "more" time are to steal time away from "non-essential" activities such as sleep or to engage in several activities at once. E.K. Scheuch uses the term "time deepening" to describe the phenomenon that is endemic to industrial societies where individuals try to accomplish several tasks at once.[13]

An example of time deepening is found in how women who work full-time and have families find ways to stretch their days. One study, conducted by the University of Wisconsin asked women to keep diaries of their day, being careful to record *all* their activities even when they were doing two things simultaneously, such as cooking dinner and helping a child with homework. The diaries revealed that the average employed mother logged nearly 33 hours and 50 minutes of accomplishments each 24 hour day.[14] For nearly twelve hours of the day, the average working mother was juggling two responsibilities simultaneously. And since the Wisconsin study predated the mobile telephone, the figures today are probably higher.

The twin problems of time deepening and cheating on sleep are interrelated. The greater the whirlwind of activity in the hours just before bedtime, the less likely one is to rest when they finally do get to bed. Perhaps the best remedy for both problems is to end each day with a period of personal meditation, not only to unwind from the day's hectic pace, but to make relaxation more likely. One physician told me that in the two decades he had been practicing medicine he found the recommendation of ending work earlier and having a period of meditation before bedtime to be more effective than sleeping medication for insomnia.

The hurried pace of our lives can even trickle down to our children resulting in their inability to sleep. When our daughter was only six years old, she experienced a time when she was too restless to sleep. Our pediatrician's advice was to let her recite the events of her day to one of us while lying in her bed. Taking her doctor's advice, for nearly a year, she would call one of us and say "Let's talk about the day." It was her way of dealing with stress (and getting extra parental attention) that even a first grader can need at times.

Any Christian knows the spiritual benefits of a daily devotional period, and in our hurried lives, we might find that there is a physical benefit as well. The psalmist said to "Be still, and know that I am God" (Ps. 46:10). Notice that the "knowing" follows the "being still." We are "fearfully and wonderfully made," (Ps. 139:14) according to David the psalmist, but all too often, we take advantage of our God-given resilience to cheat on rest and relaxation, which will eventually destroy the magnificent "temple" that we each possess. In one of the sternest warnings of the entire New Testament, Paul reminds the Corinthians "Don't you know that you yourselves are God's temple and that God's spirit lives in you? If anyone destroys God's temple, *God will destroy him*; for God's temple is sacred, and you are that temple" (1 Cor. 3:16-17).

In the light of Paul's writing, listening to our bodies and treating them with respect is much more than simply a good idea, it is a command of God.

Endnotes

1. Jeremy Rifkin, *Time Wars* (New York: Touchstone Books, 1987), p. 47.

2. *Ibid.*, p. 57.

3. Anne B. Fisher, "Welcome to the Age of Overwork." *Fortune*, November 30, 1992, pp. 64-71.

4. Natalie Angier, "Cheating on sleep: Modern life turns America into the land of the drowsy." *New York Times*, May 15, 1990, pp. C1, 8.

5. *Ibid.*, p. C1.

6. *Ibid.*, p. C8.

7. *Ibid.*

8. Jeremy Rifkin, *Time Wars*, p. 47.

9. Natalie Angier, "Cheating on sleep," p. C8.

10. *Ibid.*

11. Juliet P. Schor, *The Overworked American* (New York: Basic Books, 1991.

12. Schor cited in John Sweeny, and Karen Nussbaum, *Solutions for the Work Force* (Washington, DC: Seven Locks Press, 1989).

13. E.K. Scheuch, "The time budget interview." In A. Szalai, ed. *The Use of Time* (The Hague: Mouton, 1972).

14. H.L. Steves, and L. Bostian, "Diary and questionnaire survey of Wisconsin and Illinois employed women." *Bulletin No. 41* (1980). Madison: University of Wisconsin.

CHAPTER ELEVEN

ROUTINE MAINTENANCE IN A NON-ROUTINE WORLD

Imagine you're seated on a plane waiting to taxi away from the gate. As you prepare for your flight, the voice of the pilot comes over the intercom of the plane.

"Ladies and gentlemen," he says, "By the end of this trip you will have been a part of history. During this flight, this aircraft will set a record for most consecutive miles flown without stopping for routine maintenance."

What thoughts would go through your mind? Would you be thrilled to be a part of aviation history or terrified that you might become an aviation statistic?

The idea of letting an important machine like a passenger aircraft go without maintenance is ludicrous. However, it is equally ludicrous to let the most important and delicately made machine — the human body — go without maintenance. Yet we do it all the time.

Whatever "maintenance" you wish to mention — sleep, diet, exercise, time off — Americans are taking shortcuts. A recent Roper poll showed that in the fifteen previous years, our free time had fallen by 40%. In addition, the amount of time we take off for vacations, sick days and holidays has also decreased by three and a half days per year. At the same time, nearly half of all workers polled in a different survey said they valued leisure over work.

The two poll results tell us what we already intuitively know: we talk a good game of leisure but we rarely play it for real. By working overtime, working through lunch, taking work home and ignoring vacations, Americans "squeeze" an extra month of work into a year. It seems that we're running the engine longer and harder without any thought of the inevitable crash that will occur.

When we talk about vacations, sleeping, or just slowing down, what we are really talking about is recreation – the routine maintenance of the human body and mind. While we have turned the term recreation into a synonym for having a good time, its original meaning is simply to "re-create" one's self.

The goal of recreation is to recharge the batteries that are spent. As I write this passage, I am in the mountains of New Mexico, among some of God's greatest natural wonders, the Rocky Mountains. I'm working thanks to the "miracle" of a notebook computer. But lest you think I am a workaholic, let me tell you the pact I have made with myself. Though electricity is readily available in the cabin, I am writing with battery power that will last about two and one-half hours before it needs to be recharged. My pact is this: when the batteries in the computer need to be recharged, so do mine. And the work is put away until the next day when I have a fresh computer battery and a fresh mind.

That, in a microcosm, is what recreation is about. Not about retreating to the mountains, but about recharging your batteries wherever you are.

One of the reasons why we overwork is that it is easy to get by with it at first. Just like the airliner that doesn't crash the first time it goes without routine maintenance, our bodies don't crash the first time we work through a week-end, or ignore a week of accrued vacation. But the seeds of damage are planted.

John Maxwell compares the mismanagement of time to putting off changing the oil in your car. He says:

> If you don't change your oil every 3,000 miles your car will still start and run. The doors will still open, and the brakes will work. You're getting away with it!
>
> But after 8,000 or 10,000 miles, the engine oil has been saturated with dirt. Those particles are now grinding like sandpaper at the lining of the cylinders, pistons, and rings. Eventually the metal wears to the point that the car burns oil, the engine knocks. Left unattended, an engine designed to run over 130,000 miles is ready for the junk yard in 80,000 miles.[1]

When I first read that passage, I made a mental note to check the oil in each of my cars as soon as possible. That's the type of person I am. Later it sunk in that Maxwell was not adding an item to my personal "To Do" list. He was admonishing me to take care of myself *at least* as well as I take care of my car and preferably better. But my own routine maintenance is easy to overlook. I overwork, eat poorly or not at all, and otherwise cheat on the care of my body. But because the doors haven't fallen off (yet), I don't sweat it.

A 1993 story in *Fortune* magazine showed John Sculley, then-chairman of Apple Computer, watching a cable television business channel at 3:30 a.m. Sculley had been quoted in earlier interviews as saying that sleeping through the night is "a remnant of the agricultural or industrial age." Asked about that earlier quote, he told the *Fortune* interviewer: "People don't live that way anymore. It's a 24-hour day, not an 8-to-5 day."[2]

Many see success stories like Sculley and others and imagine that they are where they are *because* of their sleep habits, not *in spite* of them. Researcher Robert Reinheimer of Duke University, responding to Sculley's remarks in the *Fortune* article, told *USA Today* that executives such as

Sculley may be negative role models: "Technology is about using your time more efficiently so you don't have to give up five hours of sleep a night." His opinion of the sleep schedule of Sculley and others: "That's borderline nuts."[3] And often for naught. Within months of granting the interview to *Fortune*, Sculley was gone, forced out by his board.

The drive to succeed has led many to give up on leisure. More than twenty-five years ago, economist Roy Harrod warned that we may be faced with a "consumption maximum," reaching the end of our limit to enjoy the goods and services that our relatively high incomes allow because of the increasing scarcity of time left to enjoy them.[4] An illustration of Harrod's point can be seen in an article in a hobby magazine entitled "Time — Is There Ever Enough?"[5] In the article, a collector of antiques laments that the tremendous amount of time spent building an antique collection often leaves no time for enjoying them. Barbra Streisand's well-publicized 1994 art and furniture auction is a good example of this. The auction occurred because the singer wanted to "simplify" her life and get rid of many of the things she had acquired that she no longer had time to enjoy.

If we're too busy to find time for the most routine maintenance functions, such as taking a full lunch hour or getting a full night's sleep, it is almost a given that we have no time for "luxuries" such as a hobby or a day off, no matter how much we earn. This means that the fruit of our labor spoils before we stop to enjoy it. More than twenty-five years ago, this principle was noted by Staffan Linder in *The Harried Leisure Class*:

> If one has no time during a whole week to drink coffee, then obviously even whole sacks full of coffee will give no yield that week. Similarly, a tennis player has no use for a new racket each year, if he never has the time to play. The utility of theatre tickets cannot be established without knowing whether or not the ticket holder has time to use them.[6]

Television sets are a good example of the principle of reaching our collective "consumption maximum." More than two-thirds of all homes are multiple television households, yet in those households there is no more time available to watch television than in the single-television homes. The viewing merely gets spread "thinner" to a current average of only 1.5 viewers per set. Add in a VCR, a boat, a cabin in the country and you get the image of a nation of people who own more things than we can possibly stop and enjoy. In addition, the problem is worsened by all the servicing, maintenance work and security considerations required of owners of consumable goods.

According to Amy Saltzman, whose book *Downshifting* chronicles the lives of several baby boomers who had left the fast track, maintenance activities and re-creating ourselves have become another "chore" to be worked into a crowded schedule.[7]

> Leisure is just one more rushed, overscheduled obligation, often performed while we are doing something else. We read the newspaper while riding our exercise bike; we hold a meeting over our car phone while wolfing down a take-out sandwich.

Eventually the hassles of relaxing exceed the rewards, and many Americans simply forego the attempt altogether, running their internal engines without recreation for days or even months at a time.

Christian lecturer Rick Warren identifies three types of time all of us must balance: "grind" time, "prime" time and "unwind" time. Grind time is when we do what we must do. If the lawn needs mowing — it's grind time. Likewise with a project at work that requires our immediate attention. Prime time is that time when we are doing what is most important to our lives — when we "press on toward the goal," as Paul puts it in Philippians 3:14. Our daily devotion time or quality time with our families are examples of prime time activities. Finally, unwind time is when we relax and recreate. Unwind time is where we pursue a hobby, read for pleasure, exercise or engage in any other activity that relaxes us and renews us for the next grind time ahead.

Unfortunately, grind time seems to get more than its share of our daily schedules. Look back over the last week and see how many of your activities fit into the "have to" mode that characterizes grind time. Naturally your work hours fit that mode as we seek to "grind" out a living. But how many *more* activities than your normal work week also made it into grind time? Conversely, how much time did you spend in prime time, for example, in prayer and devotion to God? How much time did you spend unwinding from the stress of the week? Grind time will take over a schedule unless we safeguard against it.

Ironically, that love of grind time known as workaholism is not only an acceptable addiction in society, but a rewarded one, according to Diane Fassel, author of *Working Ourselves to Death*. She points out that John Tower was defeated in his confirmation bid for secretary of defense partially because of his alleged problems with alcohol. The same committee then endorsed Dick Cheney for the job, a man who at age 48 had already had three heart attacks and a man who acknowledged that in his role as a public servant he once worked six straight months with only one day off. "Cheney appears to have the same addictive process disease as Tower, only a different form of it," Fassel says. "Can there be any doubt that workaholism is the cleanest of all addictions?" she asks.[8]

The often-told illustration of the frog in hot water makes an appropriate point here. Throw a frog into a pot of boiling water and it will hop right back out to safety. But place a frog in a pot of room temperature water, then slowly heat it to boiling and the frog will stay in until it dies.

So it is with us. We didn't get thrown into our stifling schedules all at once or we would have recoiled in horror. More likely we slowly took on more and more responsibilities, never letting anything go as we added. Eventually we ended up over our heads. The only way out was to try to create the twenty-five hour day, the eight-day week, the fifty-three week year. And when we couldn't, we did the next best thing, we "stole" time from other places – recreation, devotion, family life, and hobbies. And like the frog, we found that one day it was too late to hop out.

Endnotes

1. John Maxwell, "Overcoming Procrastination." In Greg Asimakoupoulos, John Maxwell, and Steve McKinley, *The Time Crunch* (Sisters, OR: Multnomah Books, 1993), p. 39.

2. Alan Deutschman, "Odd man out." *Fortune*, July 26, 1993, p. 42.

3. Kevin Maney, "Information age executives not hung up on sleep." *USA Today*, July 6, 1993, Sec. C, p. 1.

4. Roy Harrod, Untitled report. In *Problems of United States Economic Development, Vol. I* (Washington, DC: Committee for Economic Development, 1958), pp. 207-213.

5. Harry Rinker, "Time – Is There Ever Enough?" *Antiques and Collecting Hobbies*, December, 1991, pp. 28-30.

6. Staffan B. Linder, *The Harried Leisure Class* (New York: Columbia University Press, 1970), p.8.

7. Amy Saltzman, *Downshifting* (New York: HarperCollins, 1991), p. 58.

8. Diane Fassel, *Working Ourselves to Death* (New York: HarperCollins, 1990), p. 120.

*"Dost thou love life?
Then do not squander time,
for that's the stuff life is made of."*
Ben Franklin

CHAPTER TWELVE

TAMING THE "ONE-EYED MONSTER"

Any discussion of time usage must eventually address the problem of the media and its influence on time consumption in the American culture. It seems strange to me that the amount of time the media consumes in our lives is rarely an issue. In speaking with parents across the nation about the topic of children and television during the writing of *The Electronic Millstone,* I discovered that conversations and concerns about the media usually gravitated toward the appropriateness of specific programs, tapes or movies. And parents are rightfully concerned about the topics of many television shows.

However, I think we are asking the wrong question. *Whether to watch* television in many families is too often assumed, and *what to watch* seems to be the only debatable issue. As Christians, however, *that* we watch is at least as important as *what* we watch. When one watches television, other possibilities are not chosen. Scores of potential activities vanish in the flickering light of the television set. Our own lives get put on hold as we watch others live their more interesting lives before us on television. *Entertainment Weekly* in a review for a fall 1994 program, called it one of television's "choicest ironies" that it could "compel entire families to sit in front of the set, watching other families be active and adventurous." As sad as that fact is, consider this: the average set has only 1.5 viewers in front of it. In reality, the more poignant irony is that the family watching others live their lives is doing so from two or three different points in the house.

The average household television is on *more than seven hours daily*. More than one-third of all households are "constant television" households where *the television never goes off* if anyone is at home. The current generation of children watches twice as much television as their parents did. From preschool until adolescence, children watch an average of more than 25 hours per week. One study revealed that one quarter of all school-age children are still watching television at 10 p.m. on a school night while another study showed that one million children under the age of eighteen were still watching television at midnight on any given school night.

By the time they turn eighteen, most children will have spent fifty percent more time with television than they spend in school. Remember also that these are averages. Obviously many children are watching much more. This makes television the primary childhood activity after sleeping and attending school, taking up an average of half of all spare time. Even throughout adulthood, for most people, television takes up *half* of all non-sleeping, non-working hours. And since these are averages, if you watch less, it make sense that someone else is watching more.

Not that some people would realize it. Audience surveys, whether done by the television industry or academicians, show that people rarely know how much television they watch. Respondents to audience surveys tend to underreport their viewing in self-kept diaries by about one half when they are cross-checked by an electronic device. These people who underreport are not lying, they are doing what most of us do — forgetting the mostly unremarkable time we have spent with television.

For example in a 1992 survey, at a time when the *average* household television was on seven hours and two minutes daily, 96% of the respondents reported that they were watching less than that. That means that 96% of the nation thought they were below the median line. Surely some were mistaken.

A number of studies and surveys indicate that television and the VCR may have become the babysitter of the 1990s. In a study published in *Journalism Quarterly*, mothers indicated that they used the television as a babysitter for their younger children an average of 2 hours and 18 minutes daily. Another study published in the same journal showed that among children three and a half to four years old, 19% of them were watching news programs alone, 40% watched situation comedies by themselves, 23% watched prime time dramas without adults present and 30% were viewing action adventure programming solo. A survey conducted by *Parent* magazine showed that parents could not determine who had chosen a particular television program more than one-third of the time, a good indication that no parent was present when the decision was made.

In an address to the Conference of the National Association for the Education of Young Children, educator Urie Bronfenbrenner underscored the fact that television crowds other activities out.

> The primary danger of the television set lies not so much in the behavior it produces — although there is danger there — as the behavior it prevents: the talks, the games, the family festivities and arguments through which much of the child's learning takes place and through which his character is formed. Turning on the television set can turn off the process that transforms children into people.[1]

Pete Hamil, in an article entitled "Crack and the Box," suggests that children who watch television are like addicts

— passive, anti-social and constantly wanting to live in some other world than the one they are in.[2] He makes the eerie observation that the first generation to grow up hooked on television was the first generation to fully embrace drugs even though hashish and marijuana had been a part of the counter-culture for most of the Twentieth Century.

Research by John Robinson shows that when families first acquire television in rural areas or developing nations, contact between family members becomes less frequent and more artificial. Television owners in developing nations also spent less time with friends, neighbors and extended family, such as cousins, etc., less time on homework and housework and less time reading.[3]

Journalist Linda Ellerbee writes of the how television changed her household in her book *Move On*:

> We stopped eating dinner at the dining-room table after my mother found out about TV trays. Dinner was served in time for one program and finished in time for another.
>
> During the meal we used to talk to one another. Now television talked to us. If you absolutely had to say something, you waited until the commercial, which is, I suspect, where I learned to speak in 30-second bursts.
>
> Before television, I would lie in bed at night, listening to my parents in their room saying things I couldn't comprehend. Their voices alone rocked me to sleep. Now Daddy went to bed right after the weather and Mama stayed up to see Jack Parr. I went to sleep listening to voices in my memory.
>
> Daddy stopped buying Perry Mason books. Perry was on television now, and that was so much easier for him. But it had been Daddy and Perry who'd taught me how fine it can be to read something you like.
>
> Mama and Daddy stopped going to movies. Most movies would one day show up on TV, he said.
>
> After a while, Daddy and I didn't play baseball anymore. We didn't go to ball games either, but we watched more baseball than ever.[4]

One common denominator in homes with heavy television viewing is that members can rarely remember, even after only 24 hours, what they view. This is because little planning went into the activity. Many of us fall in the trap of watching television, rather than watching specific programs. Since the average household television is on fifty hours per week, obviously, much of this viewing is random. Parents need to work at making all viewing purposeful. While this may sound like a call for only educational television, that is not the case. Relaxation, amusement, and family time are all good purposes. Television viewing that is purposeful, by definition, is limited. Once the purpose has been accomplished, the television is turned off.

Many parents have adopted strategies for limiting and monitoring television viewing. Some plan viewing at the beginning of each week, limiting viewing either by total hours or by quality of programming or both. New electronic devices such as TV Allowance, TV Manager, TimeSlot and others monitor the amount of television a child watches even if the parent is not home. Whatever method is used, the goal is to end the random, non-selective viewing of television whether from boredom or habit and replace it with the purposeful, limited, viewing of quality programming.

As I lectured the past four years on *The Electronic Millstone* one idea has been offered to me repeatedly. Many, but not all, parents report that when you put a limit on the *quantity* of television, the *quality* issues get taken care of. While the parent must retain veto power, most parents report that when television viewing is limited, children intuitively know which programs are junk — for instance cheaply animated afternoon cartoons — and will choose to spend their limited time on more quality programming.

Author Marie Winn, in *Unplugging the Plug-In Drug*, advocates a temporary "vacation" from television. In 1974, she organized the Denver No-TV Experiment, where families responded to her appeal to put away television for a month in order to participate in her study. What she found in this study and in replications at other sites in 1977 and 1985 was that the families reported better communication, a more peaceful atmosphere, greater closeness, more leisurely meals, more interesting conversations, more real play among the children and improved relations between the parents.[5] A quarter of the families in her experiment did not bring television back into their homes immediately after the study, preferring their new lifestyle to their old.

In an interesting follow up, when a Detroit newspaper offered families $500 to participate in a similar study for a possible feature article on life without television, the project had to be scrapped. The newspaper did not get enough takers in the entire metropolitan area to conduct the experiment. It's little wonder then that *TV Guide* reported that less than a quarter of its respondents said they would give up television permanently for a million dollars.

It is chilling to note that the things the families in the Winn study "found" when they gave up television are the same ones that the families in John Robinson's studies "lost" when television came in. Since most baby boomers cannot remember a time without television, few can grasp the magnitude of the trade-offs in time and relationships that television has required.

Many parents in their 50's and 60's notice that their now-grown children have distinctly different media habits than they do. They notice that their baby boomer children never turn off the television even when visitors arrive. They notice that their grandchildren are being babysat by the television. And they notice that their grown children are not reading. Ted Turner, chairman of Turner Broadcasting system told *USA Today*, "They don't read books and they don't read newspapers, I don't think. Whenever I go to their houses, I don't see a newspaper. . . . It's sad," referring to his grown children. "I know that I read three or four times as much as my children did," Turner added.

A parent at one seminar I held told the crowd that the biggest mistake he had made as a parent was to repair a broken television while his children were young. For a month, limited funds prevented him from taking the set to the shop. During that time, his children would come asking him to play board games. When the set was repaired, he assumed that they would continued to play games while watching television in the background. However, when the set was returned to the living room, the requests stopped and never happened again, he said.

A similar story was told to me by a college student. He said that when he was younger, his family had only one television and the family all watched together or not at all. As they became more affluent, more televisions cropped up, first in the dining room, then his parent's bedroom then in the children's rooms. With every additional television, the family became more fragmented. Conversations ended at the dinner table as everyone watched the news. The children no longer had to agree on a program to watch as everyone scattered to different sets to watch their favorites. The young man told the class, "I don't have a family yet, but when I do, I'm going to do things differently."

We need to begin to realize that television is not only a thief of time, it is a thief of family life as well. Here are some suggestions to help tame the "one-eyed monster."

1. *Audit your viewing*

Don't fall in the trap of thinking you watch less than everyone else. Those statistics demand that someone be in the middle. Find out if you are one of them.

2. *Don't "watch television," watch programs*

Though it may sound like a subtle difference, it is a real one. Television has no beginning and no end, programs do.

3. *Plan your viewing ahead of time*

Just like you plan your workday to maximize your time, you should plan your television viewing for the same reason. Avoid "impulse watching," or "channel surfing" to see if anything is on. Something always will be, and you will lose an evening to something you had little or no interest in.

4. *Take a "vacation" from television*

Marie Winn, in *Unplugging the Plug-In Drug*, claims that families taking her "No-TV" experiment enjoyed better conversations, more harmony in the home, more leisurely meals and improved marital relationships. See if your entire congregation will promote a "No-TV" week and then talk about the experience in Bible classes the next week.

5. *Have ample alternatives to television available*

If you limit or eliminate television on certain nights, you must be prepared to do activities with your children such as games, reading, puzzles or outdoor activities. We cannot declare the television "off limits" *and* mom and dad off limits at the same time.

6. *Record shows and watch them later*

The VCR can not only allow you to watch more selectively, you can also watch more efficiently since commercials and promos, which can be easily scanned over, are nearly a quarter of every television hour.

7. *Know and watch for the signs of television addiction*

Television addiction is a documented phenomenon with many of the same characteristics of drug, food or alcohol addictions. According to researcher Robin Smith, the following are the signs of television addiction.[6]

   a. Television functions as a sedative to ease pain, tension or anxiety.
   b. Television viewing brings no satisfaction and leaves the viewer frustrated.
   c. Addicts demonstrate an absence of selectivity in viewing.
   d. Addicts feel a loss of control over their viewing.
   e. Addicts lose a sense of time passing and express surprise at how long they have watched.
   f. Television provides meaning and purpose in the lives of addicted viewers.

g. Addicts structure their time around television's offerings.

h. Addicts feel they watch too much television and express a knowledge that they ought to do other things.

i. Addicts feel angry with themselves for giving in to television.

j. Addicts can't wait to get back to television when they've been away.

k. Addicts often try to quit cold turkey, and fail.

l. Addicts experience withdrawal symptoms when they try to quit.

Imagine a salesman arriving at your door one evening in a pre-television era. The man offers you the "free" entertainment of pictures and sounds in your home that will take you around the world without ever leaving your sofa. You'll get news, sports, entertainment. The small cost of a receiver will be more than offset by the fact that you no longer have to go to movies, you simply wait for movies to come to you. The same with ballgames.

Now, the cost of this "free" entertainment will be half of all the time you have left after work and sleep. Half of the conversations you would have had are now hushed, rushed or unspoken. Half or more of the books you would have read will go unread. You'll visit with your neighbors less. You'll call on extended family — aunts, uncles, cousins, etc. — more infrequently. The house will be a little less tidy and your children's homework might go undone or get done poorly. You'll need to get by on about 30 minutes less sleep than your neighbors who don't have television, but you'll get by. But other than that, he says, it's all free, the advertisers will take care of everything.

What kind of trade is that, you ask? That's not free, you say. The cost is too high!

But slowly and surely, that's the pact we've made with Hollywood. Research backs up everyone of those "costs" above and more. As Christians, we need to realize that the cable bill is the least of our worries when we think about the "cost" of television and other media. The true cost is paid in our most precious commodity: time.

In 1 Corinthians 10:23, the apostle Paul is calling the arguments of the Corinthians about the eating of meat sacrificed to idols into question. The words in quotation marks are theirs, the replies are his:

> "Everything is permissible" — but not everything is beneficial. "Everything is permissible" — but not everything is constructive.

The arguments that the Corinthians made about meat offered to idols can be made about our television usage: it's not specifically prohibited by scripture. But Paul says that a higher rule comes into play: Is it beneficial? Is it constructive?

Christians need to quit making our judgments about television and movies based on "Is it OK to watch?" We need to increase the standard and ask "Is it beneficial to watch?" And by doing so, we will be enjoying the best of the media while being good stewards of our time.

Endnotes

1. Urie Bronfenbrenner, "Who cares for America's Children?" Address to the Conference of the National Association for the Education of Young Children (1970).

2. Pete Hamil, "Crack and the Box: Television Helps Pave the Way to Addiction." *Esquire*, May, 1990, pp. 66-69.

3. John Robinson, "TV's effects on family use of time." In Jennings Bryant (Ed.) *Television and the American family* (Hillsdale, NJ: Lawrence Erlbaum Associates, Inc., 1990).

4. Linda Ellerbee, *Move On: Adventures in the Real World* (New York: G.P. Putnam's Sons, 1991).

5. Marie Winn, *The Plug-in Drug* (New York: Viking Penguin, Inc., 1987).

6. Robin Smith, "Television addiction." In Bryant, Jennings and Zillmann, D. (Eds.) *Perspectives on media effects* (Hillsdale, NJ: Lawrence Erlbaum Associates, Inc., 1988), pp. 109-128.

"Time, like an ever rolling stream,
Bears all its sons away."
Isaac Watts

CHAPTER THIRTEEN

"REDEEMING THE TIME": GETTING A HANDLE ON YOUR SCHEDULE

What is your idea of a "perfect" day? *USA Today* asked a number of experts and determined that the average American would need 42 hours a day to accomplish everything in a given day that experts say is required of the well-rounded, health-conscious individual of the 1990s. This includes 30 minutes for exercise, 45 minutes for personal grooming, two to four hours with the children and spouse, 45 minutes to read the newspapers, one and a half hours commuting, seven to ten hours working, one to two hours on housekeeping and chores, 50 minutes for intimacy, plus time for such activities as cooking and eating dinner, indulging in a hobby, reading a book, listening to music and sleeping.

Since no one has 42 hours to have a "perfect" day, the temptation is to settle for much less than we need to. In a world that is constantly threatening our ability to re-create ourselves, we must make an effort to relax and enjoy our God-given blessings. Here are some practical tips.

1. *Know your "Plimsoll mark" and honor it*

In *The Time Crunch*, the authors relate a story that prior to the Merchant Shipping Act of 1876, several heavily-loaded English vessels had sunk resulting in loss of life and cargo due to being overloaded. Compounding the problem was the fact that the owners of the ships were heavily insured from any losses, giving them little motivation to solve the problem.

Prompted by Samuel Plimsoll, the English Parliament enacted the Merchant Shipping Act of 1876. Among other things, the Act established a requirement that all merchant vessels have a load line painted on the hull that would be visible above the water only if the ship's weight was safe. The line became known as the "Plimsoll mark."

Each of us has an internal Plimsoll mark, and intuitively, each of us knows where our mark is. The trouble is not that the demands of our employment alone take us to that mark. That is rarely the case. More likely, those who are "drowning" in obligations are driven there by the cumulative effect of jobs, parenting, church work, clubs and organizations, and the like. Others are "drowning" in debt, which requires that they take on second jobs.

Whether we are drowning in obligations or debt or both, the secret to keeping our personal "Plimsoll mark" above the sinking level is self-control. When we say yes to one more committee when our common sense and our calendars scream "No!" the line gets lower. When we join the growing numbers who won't take a vacation this year or a day off this week, we're loading the boat of our lives lower and lower. Eventually we drown or "burn out" to use a more common metaphor.

Try this exercise. At least once a year, look at all of your standing obligations and see which ones, if any, you can eliminate. Then, having pared your obligations down to the essentials, don't take on any more without letting something go. We are constantly asked to add another worthwhile obligation — chairing a school committee, coaching a soccer team, teaching a Bible class — without dropping any of the other myriad of balls we are juggling. Sooner or later what comes crashing down is our health.

2. *Take a trickle charge*

Remember that notebook computer in Chapter 11 that needed recharging after about two and one-half hours? As with most computers there are two ways to recharge it. The first, and fastest, is to turn it off and let it recharge. However, I sometimes can't spare the computer that long. In those instances, I plug it into the wall and charge it as I use it. In the jargon, it's called a "trickle charge." Between doing the work it has to do, my computer is recharging itself for the next project.

Often that is what we are forced to do. In the absence of an all-out, turn-me-off-and-plug-me-in vacation, we must take a "trickle charge." Greg Asimakoupoulos, pastor and Christian author, writes of taking a "sabbatical" in the office.[1] Realizing that he badly needed a time of rejuvenation and realizing that his circumstances would not allow a several week sabbatical, Greg set out to take a sabbatical without leaving town. During that time, and with the consent of his board, he pared down his "To Do" list to the bare essentials. First, he caught up on lost sleep. Then he began to exercise an hour a day, spent more time in meditation and devotion, and even renewed an old hobby of photography. In short, he returned to a schedule more suited to the human condition than the one to which he'd grown accustomed. He returned from his reduced schedule feeling "more loved and accepted by God than at any time in my ministry."

You're probably already thinking: my job wouldn't last if I gave it less than 110% fifty-plus weeks a year. And perhaps you're right. Greg's solution was peculiar to his situation, yet all of us can find a way to take a trickle charge. For many it could be a half-week vacation. In a 1987 study, Marriott Corporation found that trips of three days or less accounted for 73% of vacations taken by those surveyed.[2] The amount of time is irrelevant — the need is not. Howard Thurman, in *The Inward Journey*, recommends "minute vacations" during the day. Minute vacations are a chance to retreat from the present and put yourself into a less worried, less hectic posture and mental state, even if only for a minute. You can call it "kicking back" or "putting your feet up," but under any name, it works.

In the middle of one of the busiest periods of my life, with three small children, a full-time teaching job, a full load at graduate school and writing for the local newspaper to make ends meet, I talked with a counselor who is a friend of mine about the merits of relaxation therapy. He invited me to his office to show me how he relaxed his clients for a therapy session. As background music played, he dimmed the lights and suggested that I close my eyes and pick my favorite spot in nature and put myself there.

At that time in my life, I was so wrapped up in my work that my favorite spots were my office, my reading chair at home and my carrel in the library at the university. I didn't have a single place in nature to transport my mind. Finally, I remembered a lithograph of a nature scene in my office and I "borrowed" that scene from a place I had never been as my "favorite" spot for purposes of relaxation therapy. That's when I knew that I needed more vacations — minute and otherwise. And I took them. Today when I close my eyes for a "minute vacation," I have to choose between competing spots around the world in which to place myself.

In *You Don't Have to Go Home From Work Exhausted*, Ann McGee-Cooper calls these "joy breaks" from work essential. They can be meditation, stretching exercises, calling a loved one on the phone or playing a computer game.[3] She says

> Most managers think you can't enjoy anything until after their work is done. The trouble is, these days their work is *never* really done. So without any fun in their lives, they go into a state of exhaustion and depression.[4]

3. *Strive for balance*

The longer I live, the more I'm convinced that the familiar passage in Ecclesiastes 3:1-8 is not a *suggestion*, it is a *prescription* for long life. Though it's a well-known passage, read it again.

> There is a time for everything,
> and a season for every activity under heaven:
> a time to be born and a time to die,
> a time to plant and a time to uproot,
> a time to kill and a time to heal,
> a time to tear down and a time to build,
> a time to weep and a time to laugh,
> a time to mourn and a time to dance,
> a time to scatter stones and a time to gather them,
> a time to embrace and a time to refrain,
> a time to search and a time to give up,
> a time to keep and a time to throw away,
> a time to tear and a time to mend,
> a time to be silent and a time to speak,
> a time to love and a time to hate,
> a time for war and a time for peace (Eccl. 3:1-8).

These activities *are not* a cafeteria of ways to be happy. I can't pick a couple, do them well, and expect to be happy, even though we have all known people who have made a life out of one or two items on the list. It's not good enough to do some of or even half of the things listed in this passage. We must learn to do them *all*, because the scripture tells us that *each* has its place.

Maybe you don't dance as well as you plant. In my case it's no contest: I can't dance at all. But it's not Solomon's point in this passage that I do all these activities equally well, or that I even *like* doing all of them. And I don't think that it needs to be literal dancing — any overt expression of the joy of life will do. The same with planting. You don't have to get your hands dirty to do something that examines the wonder of the universe and encourages the renewal of life. Find your approximation of each item on the list and then do it in its proportion.

The point is that a life that is all planting and no dancing is a life lived "under the sun." It's a phrase used repeatedly in Ecclesiastes 1 and 2. Life lived "under the sun" is "meaningless," and "chasing after the wind." There is no end to labor and no satisfaction in it. Never enough time. But watch what happens to life when it is lived "under heaven." As Ecclesiastes 3:1 suggests: There is a time for everything! What happened? Did the day get longer? No. In that one verse that begins Ecclesiastes 3, the measuring stick for a successful day changed: a good day is a balanced day, with enough time for every worthwhile activity under heaven, including leisure. We need to change the definition of a "full" day. It is not a day where we do a lot of one thing (for instance, work). A full day is a day where we do several things in their rightful proportion.

Research backs up what Solomon knew intuitively in his wisdom. Howard and Diane Tinsley, professors of psychology at Southern Illinois University, found that individuals experiencing "leisure" feel the following:

1. Total absorption in (or intense concentration on) the activity at hand.
2. Lack of focus on (or forgetting of) self.
3. Feelings of freedom.
4. Enriched perception of objects and events.
5. Increased sensitivity to bodily sensations.
6. Increased sensitivity to and intensity of emotions.
7. Decreased awareness of the passage of time.[5]

In short, the researchers found a freedom from the futility that marks Ecclesiastes 1 and 2 in those persons who were engaged in leisure activities. While the benefits of taking time for leisure activities are well documented, it still takes a concentrated effort for many to choose leisure activities over work.

4. *Pursue peace*

In Psalm 34:12 David asks this question: "Which of you delights in life and desires a long life to enjoy all things?"

Assuming an answer in the affirmative, he then gives a formula for long life in the next two verses, concluding with this striking remark: "seek peace and pursue it."

We need to quit thinking of peace as a by-product. Early in our adulthood we are tempted to think that peace is a by-product of financial freedom. Later we think that peace comes from having faithful, fully-grown children. Still later, we look for peace in good health and freedom from illness. And after spending a lifetime of always thinking peace is only one more good fortune away, we find too late that *peace is not a by-product of anything*, it is an end in itself. I know this to be true because Psalm 34:14 tells me to pursue it. Peace can be "caught" without catching anything else first. If peace were only possible through financial security or good health, God, speaking through the psalmist David, would have encouraged me to pursue wealth and health to get the peace that comes with it. But he didn't. He said to pursue peace.

Peace can be found in any circumstances, even when it makes no sense to have it. I think that's what Paul means in Philippians 4:7 when he talks about the "peace of God which passes all understanding." Sometimes it just doesn't make sense to seek peace in the middle of a "25-hour" day, but then again, it doesn't make sense to try to get through a "25-hour" day without a little peace either, does it?

What is your pet peeve? For me it's no contest: I hate being stuck in traffic. But for many it's a daily reality. The average urban commute is now 45 minutes one way and climbing 20% per decade. But for me that would be a nightmare. Paul tells us in Philippians 4:11: "I have learned to be content whatever the circumstances." I don't know if I will ever progress spiritually to the point where I can be content in the occasional traffic jams in which I find myself. But if I do, both the Bible and modern science agree: I'll lengthen my life. It's a promise: "Which of you delights in life and desires a long life to enjoy all things? Let him . . . seek peace and pursue it."

5. *Learn the gift of enjoyment*

In teaching Ecclesiastes to a group of university students at my congregation one quarter, I ran across a startling concept in the fifth chapter: *the ability to enjoy myself is a gift from God.* In Ecclesiastes 5:19, Solomon says, "Moreover, it is a gift of God that every man to whom he has granted wealth and riches and the power to enjoy them should accept his lot and rejoice in his labor."

For years, I had no problem with the last half of that verse. I rejoiced in my work and I met the goals I set for myself. But it dawned on me as I prepared that class that I almost totally lacked the gift of enjoyment. I was blessed with the gift of *accomplishment* but not the gift of *enjoyment*. This deficit meant that no matter what I did, it was never enough. And then I realized that if the ability to enjoy is a gift, then it can be acquired through prayer and willingness to change. I am assured in 1 Timothy 6:17 that God has given me all things to enjoy. The challenge is to learn to enjoy them. I prayed about it for a long time, and though I still have room for improvement, I can say that I am better today at enjoying my blessings than ever before.

In my research, I have noticed that the inability to enjoy was not a peculiar phenomenon. In fact, it was a quite common one among successful individuals, some of whom have low self-esteem despite their many accomplishments. Fueled by a constant need to be reminded of their worth, these individuals trudge on to more accomplishments, seldom pausing to enjoy the achievements of the present. In one of my interviews, a highly successful individual told me that he actually prayed to God to "turn down the intensity level" of his life. He had recognized that he was totally powerless by himself to step off the treadmill he was on, but with God's help, he hoped to break the cycle. If you are one of those individuals who have trouble stopping to enjoy, remember that it's a gift of God promised to you. But like all gifts, it must be accepted.

One final note to end this chapter: the computer battery

ran out half an hour ago and I finished the chapter by plugging in the computer and taking a "trickle charge." Sometimes it's easier to give advice than to take it.

Endnotes

1. Greg Asimakoupoulos, "A Sabbatical in the Office." In Greg Asimakoupoulos, John Maxwell, and Steve McKinley, eds. *The Time Crunch* (Sisters, Oregon: Multnomah Books, 1993), pp. 138-145.

2. Amy Saltzman, *Downshifting* (New York: Harper Collins, 1991), p. 22.

3. Ann McGee-Cooper, *You Don't Have to Go Home From Work Exhausted* (Dallas: Bowen and Rogers Publishing, 1990).

4. Anne B. Fisher, "Welcome to the Age of Overwork." *Fortune*, November 30, 1990, pp. 64-71.

5. Saltzman, *Downshifting*, p. 208.

CHAPTER FOURTEEN
_____
THE GIFT OF REST

One of the indictments of Israel found in the writings of the prophet Isaiah is that the people did not take the rest which God offered them. Isaiah 28:12 tells us that God said "This is the resting place, let the weary rest" but the people would not listen. In that same chapter Isaiah condemns them for having made "a covenant with death."

Are we guilty of the same thing? Do we repeatedly pass up God's offer of a place to rest and run recklessly towards an early rendezvous with death? Can we even find God's resting place? David gives us a clue when he says "I will lie down and sleep in peace for you alone, O Lord, make me dwell in safety" (Ps. 4:8). Our resting place is found in God. It's a relationship, not a location. I like the words of this hymn by Cleland B. McAfee that addresses the question of where we turn for rest.

> There is a place of quiet rest
> Near to the heart of God
> A place where sin cannot molest
> Near to the heart of God

> There is a place of comfort sweet
> Near to the heart of God
> A place where we our Savior meet
> Near to the heart of God.

I think that one reason why we hurry so much has little to do with economic necessity. I think it's that we fear that if we get still we might have to meet God and come to grips with what are lives have become. As long as we're on the treadmill, we have no time for introspection. But if things ever get still, we must face the God who wants an accounting of how we are spending His time.

In less than a week I will be teaching nearly fifty new college freshmen, most of them away from home for the first time. The first few weeks they'll look scared. After that, they'll simply look tired as they get into a pattern of too many activities and too little sleep. They will form the habits of an adult lifetime on my campus, yet nothing in our catalog, our curriculum or our calendar is preparing them to learn to rest. Where will they learn it?

One final quotation from Isaiah 30:15 is particularly troublesome to me. God, speaking to his people says,

> In repentance and rest is your salvation,
> in quietness and trust is your strength,
> but you would have none of it.

Even though they were surrounded by hostile nations, Israel's salvation was not in its armies. Israel's salvation was contingent on first turning back to God and then accepting His rest. Yet the passage goes on to say that they chose to flee on swift horses rather than accept those two conditions. They trusted in their horses rather than their God.

God's offer of salvation to us is also an offer of rest. In Matthew 11:28–30 Jesus makes this offer:

> Come to me, all you who are weary and burdened and I
> will give you rest. Take my yoke upon you and learn from

me, for I am gentle and humble in heart, and you will find rest for your souls. For my yoke is easy and my burden is light.

What kind of "swift horses" will we saddle and ride before we accept his simple offer? For some it will be wealth. For others it will be fame. Some of us will take up his offer as soon as we have enough saved away for retirement. Others will wait until our children are grown.

And what will we miss while we are riding our "swift horses?" A baby's first steps? A school play? Watching a son hit his first home run? Sending a daughter off for her first real date?

Like Jonah who found a boat or the children of Israel who mounted up on swift horses, we will always find a vehicle we can ride away from God. But we will never do better than His offer of a yoke that is easy and a burden that is light in exchange for rest for our souls.

I finish this book as I started: a flawed messenger for the topic. I do not yet juggle all of my responsibilities well. A few balls drop every now and then. But I learn, pick up and go on.

My final illustration comes from my favorite American play, Thornton Wilder's "Our Town." It's a play within a play, directed along by the ever-present Stage Manager. In the last act, Emily, who has died in childbirth, asks the Stage Manager if she can go back and relive a single day. He consents, but warns her to pick an insignificant one, hoping to lessen her disappointment. Once back among the living, however, she stays for only a few minutes before she asks to be taken away again. The indifference her living mother and father showed towards the preciousness of life was too much for the recently-deceased Emily to take. They were living the day precisely as they had lived it the "first" time, but Emily, from her perspective, could see now how little they appreciated the gift of life.

"Does anyone realize life while they're living it?" she

asks the Stage Manager. "Only a few," he replies. "Saints and a few poets." I close this book with the hope that the vision of saints and poets will come to you, and that you will realize that every day is a special gift from God. No day is insignificant and no day can be lived again.

SUGGESTED RESOURCES
AND BIBLIOGRAPHY

Suggested Readings:

Covey, Stephen. *The 7 Habits of Highly Effective People*. New York: Simon and Schuster (1989).

Fassel, Diane. *Working Ourselves to Death*. San Francisco: HarperCollins (1990).

Hewlett, Sylvia Ann. *When the Bough Breaks*. New York: Basic Books (1991).

Hochschild, Arlie. *The Second Shift*. New York: Viking Penguin (1989).

Keyes, Ralph. *Timelock*. New York: HarperCollins (1991).

Rifkin, Jeremy. *Time Wars*. New York: Henry Holt (1987).

Saltzman, Amy. *Downshifting*. New York: HarperCollins (1991).

Schor, Juliet P. *The Overworked American*. New York: Basic Books (1991).

Smith, Malcolm. *Spiritual Burnout*. Tulsa: Honor Books (1988).

Young, Helen and Silvey, Billie. *Time Management for Christian Women*. Nashville: Twenty-first Century Christian (1990).

Additional Resources:

Consultation: Workaholics Anonymous
511 Sir Francis Drake C-170
Greenbrae, CA 94904

Seminars: Dr. Philip D. Patterson
2501 E. Memorial Rd.
Box 11000
Oklahoma City, OK 73136

Bibliography

Books:

Albert, Linda and Michael Popkin. *Quality Parenting*. New York: Random House, 1987.

Cahn, Edgar and Jonathan Rowe. *Time Dollars*. Emmaus, PA: Rodale Press, 1991.

Covey, Stephen. *The 7 Habits of Highly Effective People*. New York: Simon and Schuster, 1989.

Elkind, David. *Grandparenting*. New York: Scott, Foresman and Company, 1990.

Ellerbee, Linda. *Move On*. New York: G.P. Putnam's Sons, 1991.

Fassel, Diane. *Working Ourselves to Death*. San Francisco: HarperCollins, 1990.

Fuchs, Victor R. *Women's Quest for Economic Equality*. Cambridge, MA: Harvard University Press, 1988.

Gutmann, David. *Reclaimed Powers*. New York: Basic Books, 1987.

Hewlett, Sylvia Ann. *When the Bough Breaks*. New York: Basic Books, 1991.

Hochschild, Arlie. *The Second Shift*. New York: Viking Penguin, 1989.

Kanter, Rosabeth M. *When Giants Learn to Dance*. New York: Simon & Schuster, 1989.

Keyes, Ralph. *Timelock*. New York: HarperCollins, 1991.

Kubey, Robert and Mihaly Csikszentmihalyi. *Television and the Quality of Life*. Hillsdale, NJ: Lawrence Erlbaum Associates, 1990.

Linder, Steffan B. *The Harried Leisure Class*. New York: Columbia University Press, 1970.

Marrus, Michael R., ed. *The Emergence of Leisure*. New York: Harper Torchbooks, 1974.

Massachusetts Mutual. *Massachusetts Mutual Family Values Study*. Washington, DC: Mellman & Lazarus Inc., 1989.

McGee-Cooper, Ann. *You Don't Have to Go Home From Work Exhausted*. Dallas: Bowen and Rogers Publishing, 1990.

Mishel, Lawrence, and Jacqueline Simon. *The State of Working America*. Armonk, NY: M.E. Sharpe, 1990.

O'Malley, Michael. *Keeping Watch*. New York: Viking, 1990.

Patterson, Philip. *Come Unto Me*. Joplin, MO: College Press Publishing, 1993.

Postman, Neil. *Amusing Ourselves to Death*. New York: Penguin Books, 1986.

Rifkin, Jeremy. *Time Wars*. New York: Henry Holt, 1987.

Robinson, John P., Vladimir G. Andreyenkov, and Vasily D. Patrushev. *The Rhythm of Everyday Life*. Boulder: Westview Press, 1988.

Saltzman, Amy. *Downshifting*. New York: HarperCollins, 1991.

Schlosstein, Steven. *The End of the American Century*. Chicago: Congdon and Weed, 1989.

Schor, Juliet P. *The Overworked American*. New York: Basic Books, 1991.

Smith, Malcolm. *Spiritual Burnout*. Tulsa: Honor Books, 1988.

Stinnett, Nick and John DeFrain. *Secrets of Strong Families*. Boston: Little, Brown, 1985.

Sweeny, John J. and Karen Nussbaum. *Solutions for the Workforce*. Washington, DC: Seven Locks Press, 1989.

Weitzman, Lenore. *The Divorce Revolution*. New York: The Free Press, 1985.

Winn, Marie. *The Plug-in Drug*. New York: Viking Penguin, Inc., 1987.

Young, Helen and Billie Silvey. *Time Management for Christian Women*. Nashville: Twenty-first Century Christian, 1990.

Zelizer, Viviana A. 1985. *Pricing the Priceless Child*. New York: Basic Books.

Chapters:

Asimakoupoulos, Greg. "A Sabbatical in the Office" in Greg Asimakoupoulos, John Maxwell, and Steve McKinley, eds. *The Time Crunch*. Sisters, Oregon: Multnomah Books, 1993, pp. 138-145.

Maxwell, John. "Overcoming Procrastination" in Greg Asimakoupoulos, John Maxwell, and Steve McKinley, eds. *The Time Crunch*. Sisters, OR: Multnomah Books, 1993, pp. 35-50.

Robinson, John. "TV's effects on family use of time" in Bryant Jennings, ed. *Television and the American Family*. Hillsdale, NJ: Lawrence Erlbaum Associates, Inc., 1990.

Scheuch, E. K. "The time budget interview" in A. Szalai, ed. *The Use of Time*. The Hague: Mouton, 1972.

Smith, Robin. "Television addiction" in Bryant Jennings and D. Zillmann, eds. *Perspectives on Media Effects*. Hillsdale, NJ: Lawrence Erlbaum Associates, Inc., 1988, pp. 109-128.

Timmer, S.G., J. Eccles, and K. O'Brien. "How children use their time" in F.G. Juster and F.P. Stafford, eds. *Time, Goods and Well-being*. Ann Arbor: University of Michigan Press, 1985, pp. 352-382.

Government documents

Harrod, Roy. Untitled report. In *Problems of United States Economic Development, Vol. I*. Washington, DC: Committee for Economic Development, 1958, pp. 207-213.

Select Committee on Children, Youth and Families. *Eating Disorders: The Impact on Children and Families* Washington, DC: U.S. House of Representatives, 1987, p. 3.

Steves, H. L. and L. Bostian. *Diary and Questionnaire Survey of Wisconsin and Illinois Employed Women*. (Bulletin No. 41). Madison: University of Wisconsin, 1980.

Studies in Marriage and the Family 1989. *Current Population Reports Series P-23, No. 162*. Washington, DC: U.S. Bureau of the Census, p. 5.

Journals

Coombs, Robert H. and John Landsverk. "Parenting Styles and Substance Use During Childhood and Adolescence." *Journal of Marriage and the Family*, 50 (1988), pp. 473-482.

Eggebeen, David and Peter Uhlenberg. "Changes in the Organization of Men's Lives: 1960-1980." *Family Relations, 34* (1985), p. 255.

Lehrer. Joel F. and Leila M. Hover. "Fatigue Syndrome." *Journal of the American Medical Association*, 259 (1983), pp. 842-843.

Mattox, William R. Jr. "The Family Time Famine." *Family Policy, 3* (1990), p. 2.

_____. "The Parent Trap: So Many Bills, So Little Time." *Policy Review, 55* (Winter, 1991), pp. 6-13.

Merskey, Helen S. and G.T. Swart. "Family Background and Physical Health of Adolescents Admitted to an Inpatient Psychiatric Unit." *Canadian Journal of Psychiatry, 34* (1989), pp. 79-83.

National Association of Elementary School Principals Staff Report. "One-Parent Families and Their Children." *Principal, 60* (September, 1980), pp. 31-37.

Velez, Carmen Noemi and Patricia Cohen. "Suicidal Behavior and Ideation in a Community Sample of Children: Maternal and Youth Reports." *Journal of the American Academy of Child and Adolescent Psychiatry, 27* (1988), pp. 349-356.

Watkins, Susan, Jane Menken, and John Bongaarts. "Demographic Foundations of Family Change." *American Sociological Review, 52* (1987), pp. 346-358.

Newspaper articles:

Angier, Natalie. "Cheating on sleep: Modern life turns America into the land of the drowsy." *New York Times,* May 15, 1990, pp. C1, 8.

Bennett, Amanda. "Early to Bed . . . A Look at the CEO Work-week." *Wall Street Journal*, March 20, 1987, p. 22D.

Burtless, Gary. "Are We All Working Too Hard? It's Better Than Watching Oprah." *Wall Street Journal*, January 4, 1990, p. B1.

Kroeger, Brooke. "Feeling Poor on $600,000 a Year." *New York Times*, April 26, 1987, Sec. III, p. 1.

Maney, Kevin. "Information Age Executives Not Hung Up on Sleep." *USA Today*, July 6, 1993, Sec. C, p. 1.

Marvel, Bill. "Little Orphan Annie Would Hardly Recognize the Place." *Dallas Morning News*, November 28, 1991, Sec. C, pp. 1-2.

Rosenfeld, Megan. "Thanks a Bunch." *Washington Post*, November 9, 1986, p. H3.

Unknown. "We Get Little Satisfaction for Being Sofa Spuds." *Atlanta Constitution*, April 5, 1993, Sec. E, p. 1.

Yates, Ronald. "Japanese Live. . .and Die. . .for Their Work." *Chicago Tribune*, November 13, 1988, p. 1.

Periodicals:

Adler, Jerry. "Kids Growing Up Scared." *Newsweek*, January 10, 1994, pp. 43-49.

Balzer, Harry. "The Ultimate Cooking Appliance." *American Demographics*, July 1993, pp. 40-44.

Bloch, Gordon. "I Don't Have Time." *Runner's World*, January 1991, pp. 32-35.

Butler, Katy. "The Great Boomer Bust." *Mother Jones*, June 1989, pp. 32-38.

Chapman, Fern. "Executive guilt: Who's Taking Care of the Children?" *Fortune*, February 1987, pp. 30-37.

Deutschman, Alan. "Odd Man Out." *Fortune*, July 26, 1993, p. 42.

Fisher, Anne B. "Welcome to the Age of Overwork." *Fortune*, November 30, 1992, pp. 64-71.

Gibbs, Nancy. "How America Has Run Out of Time." *Time*, April 24, 1989, pp. 58-67.

Godbey, Geoffrey and Alan Graffe. "Rapid Growth in Rushin' Americans." *American Demographics*, April 1993, pp. 26-28.

Grogan, David. "Vanished — With a Trace." *People*, March 3, 1994, pp. 69-72.

Hamil, Pete. "Crack and the box: Television Helps Pave the Way to Addiction." *Esquire*, May 1990, pp. 66-69.

Hamilton, Kendall. "Not Another Pretty Face." *Newsweek*, July 25, 1994, pp. 50-51.

Hewlett, Sylvia Ann. "Running Hard Just to Keep Up." *Time*, Fall 1990, Special Issue entitled *Women: The Road Ahead,* p. 54.

Klein, Joe. "Whose Values?" *Newsweek*, June 8, 1992, pp. 19-22.

O'Reilly, Brian. "Why Grade 'A' Execs Get an 'F' as Parents." *Fortune*, January 1, 1990, pp. 36-37.

_____. "Is Your Company Asking Too Much?" *Fortune*, March 12, 1990, pp. 38-46.

McDowell, Josh. "Study Shows Church Kids Not Waiting." *Christianity Today*, March 18, 1988, pp. 54-55.

Rinker, Harry. "Time — Is There Ever Enough?" *Antiques and Collecting Hobbies*, December 1991, pp. 28-30.

Robinson, John P. "Time's Up." *American Demographics*, July 1989, pp. 32-35.

————————. "The Time Squeeze." *American Demographics*, February 1990, pp. 30-33.

————————. "Who's Doing the Housework?" *American Demographics*, December 1988, pp. 24-28.

Rock, Andrea. "Can You Afford Your Kids?" *Money*, July 1990, pp. 88-99.

Solo, Sally. "Stop Whining and Get Back to Work." *Fortune*, March 12, 1990, pp. 49-50.

Worthy, Ford S. "You're Probably Working Too Hard." *Fortune*, April 27, 1987, pp. 135-140.

Public addresses

Bronfenbrenner, Urie. "Who cares for America's Children?" Address to the Conference of the National Association for the Education of Young Children, 1970.

Faulkner, Paul. "Getting Ahead and Taking Your Children with You." Public lecture in Oklahoma City, OK, December 8, 1991.

About the Author

Philip Patterson has been a professor of journalism at Oklahoma Christian University of Science and Arts in Oklahoma City since 1981. He received his degrees from Lubbock Christian University (B.A. in Religion, 1976), Abilene Christian University (M.A. in Journalism, 1981) and the University of Oklahoma (Ph.D. in Political Communication, 1987).

Philip was awarded the Gaylord Chair of Teaching Excellence at Oklahoma Christian in 1988. In 1989, the Poynter Institute for Media Studies named him as one of the ten outstanding professors of media ethics nationally. He was named the outstanding alumnus of his alma mater, Lubbock Christian University, in 1993.

Philip has written two other books for the Christian market: *The Electronic Millstone* (1992) and *Come Unto Me* (1993). He is also the author of two college textbooks, one of them the most widely-adopted media ethics text in the nation.

He lives in Edmond, OK, with his wife, Linda who is an artist and homemaker and his children, Amy, Andrew and Joshua.